GHOST STORIES
of the
CIVIL WAR

Dan Asfar and Edrick Thay

GHOST
HOUSE

Ghost House Books

The Publisher: Ghost House Books
Distributed by Lone Pine Publishing

10145 – 81 Avenue	1808 – B Street NW, Suite 140
Edmonton, AB Canada T6E 1W9	Auburn, WA USA 98001

Website: http://www.ghostbooks.net

National Library of Canada Cataloguing in Publication Data

Asfar, Dan, 1973–
    Ghost stories of the Civil War / Dan Asfar, Edrick Thay.

    ISBN 1-894877-16-0

    1. Ghosts—United States. 2. United States—History—Civil War, 1861–1865—Miscellanea. I. Thay, Edrick, 1977– II. Title.
BF1472.U6A83 2003   133.1'0973'09034   C2003-911078-8

Editorial Director: Nancy Foulds
Project Editors: Shelagh Kubish, Chris Wangler
Editorial: Shelagh Kubish, Lindsay Parker
Researcher: Alana Bevans
Illustrations Coordinator: Carol Woo
Production Director: Gene Longson
Book Design, Layout & Production: Lynett McKell
Cover Design: Gerry Dotto

Photo Credits: Every effort has been made to accurately credit photographers. Any errors or omissions should be directed to the publisher for changes in future editions. The photographs and illustrations in this book are reproduced with the kind permission of the following sources: Library of Congress (Cover: DIG-cwpb-01109; pp. 4-5: HABS, LA,36-NEWOR,1-2; p. 11: HABS, VA,89-CHANVI,1-5; p. 13: HABS, VA,89-CHANVI, 1-4: VA; p. 16: USZC4-4587; p. 23: USZ62-107446; p. 33: B817-7411; p. 39: HABS, VA,28-HAMP,2A-3; p. 37: USZ62-108225; p. 48: HAER, GA,024-FOOG.V,1-14; p. 51: USZ62-5452; p. 54: B8171-2336; p. 56: USZ62-4892; p. 64: USZC4-1732; p. 83: B8184-10018; p. 89: USZ62-12757; p. 92: USZC4-1754; p. 97: HABS, LA,36-NEWOR,1-2; p. 100: USZ62-3583; p. 111: HABS, VA,100-YORK,1-22; p. 116: B8184-10692; p.119: D4-18558; p.132: HABS, WVA, 19-HARF, 3-4; p. 148: D4-71430; p. 160: USZ62-95101; p. 163: USZ62-122695; p. 180: DIG-cwpb-00864 p. 182: B8171-7318; p. 185: USZ62-40270; p. 200: USZ62-40260; p 205: D4-16614); Joyce Toney (p. 19); Florida Center for Instructional Technology (p. 41); John Grafton, *The Civil War*, Dover Publications (p. 144, 195); Sandusky Library (p. 3,177: JOIS–103); Chicago Historical Society (p. 211: ICHi-31103).

The stories, folklore and legends in this book are based on the authors' research of sources including individuals whose experiences have led them to believe they have encountered phenomena of some kind or another. They are meant to entertain, and neither the publisher nor the authors claim these stories represent fact.

We acknowledge the financial support of the Government of Canada through the Book Publishing Industry Development Program (BPIDP) for our publishing activities.

PC: P6

To J. T. Carson and John Herd Thompson

Contents

Acknowledgments 6
Introduction 7

Chapter One: Forts and Battlefields

Chapter Two: Haunted Houses

Acknowledgments

Thanks to all those who keep the supernatural lore of the United States alive through their work and willingness to talk. Thanks to Randy and Nancy Pichl, Sandra Skoda-Whipple and her husband Dennis. Nicole Bray and the West Michigan Ghost Hunters Society have once again proven invaluable. As well, kudos to Allie Pierce, Mary-Alison Wilshire and of course author Nancy Roberts, whose work on the subject of ghosts of the Civil War sets an impressive standard. Thanks also to Diane Nicodemus of the *Gettysburg Times*. And finally, thanks to all those individuals who came forward to talk to us about their experiences on condition of anonymity. This book would not be what it is without your accounts.

Introduction

On November 6, 1860, the people of the United States of America elected Abraham Lincoln as their president. A little more than a month later, South Carolina had seceded from the Union. By February 1861, Mississippi, Florida, Alabama, Georgia, Louisiana and Texas had followed. Together they formed the Confederate States of America, a country with its own government and a newly elected president, Jefferson Davis. They were to be joined later by Arkansas, North Carolina, Virginia and Tennessee, whose governments shared the Confederacy's love of that most peculiar institution, slavery. Determined not to come under the yoke of the United States government once again, the Confederate States of America did not take long to assert their independence and autonomy.

Under orders from Jefferson Davis, Confederate General Pierre Beauregard attacked Fort Sumter in Charleston, South Carolina. Did the leaders of the Confederacy realize what they had done? They were attempting to preserve a way of life, to maintain a freedom won in the American Revolution. Theirs was a precarious liberty, under threat now from an industrial North that sought to undermine their agrarian lifestyles. In attacking the fort, they must have known that their actions would lead to open warfare. Perhaps that was the intent. Regardless, few could have imagined the maelstrom of death that was unleashed.

In just 20 minutes, 7000 Americans died fighting at Cold Harbor, Virginia. In the bloodiest single day of the war at Antietam, 23,000 died. Over 60,000 perished on the fields of Gettysburg in the bloodiest battle of the war. For four years, the Civil War engulfed the country, its touch devastating the nation.

Economies were ruined, homes destroyed, hearts and souls shattered. More than three million men fought in the war, and 620,000 lost their lives in a steady hail of bullets, shrapnel and disease—more men than in any other single American war. In fact, more men died in the Civil War than in the Revolutionary War, the War of 1812, the Mexican War, the Spanish-American War and the two World Wars combined. The war challenged men like President Abraham Lincoln, Union General Ulysses S. Grant and Confederate General Robert E. Lee, transforming them into mythic figures. When Robert E. Lee finally surrendered his Army of Northern Virginia at Appomattox on April 9, 1865, the nation breathed a sigh of relief. The war's conclusion was near. The United States of America were once again united, at least on the surface. Lincoln's assassination on April 14, 1865, was an indication of exactly how volatile emotions were and how fragile the union was.

The Civil War is arguably *the* most important chapter in American history. Its far-reaching consequences influenced and continue to influence nearly every aspect of American life. It ended one way of life and ushered in another, eliminating the Southern planter aristocracy built upon the backs of slaves. The new economic order was predicated on big industry and bigger business.

Today, children learn about the war in school, historians debate its origins and people look to see how America was born. Those who visit the countless historical sites are always moved by what they see and learn; others might encounter one or more of the thousands of ghosts associated with the war.

Physical, and not-so-physical, remnants of the Civil War are scattered across the nation. There are thousands of sites dedicated to the memories of battles fought and lives lost. Visits to them cause people to speak in whispered tones, walking about slowly as if haste or noise would offend the lingering spirits. Perhaps they are right to be cautious. For there are spirits here, thousands of them baptized in the cauldron of war.

Tragedy often traps the spirits of the dead, keeping them on the mortal plane for whatever reason. Sometimes it is for love, other times it is for respect. Regardless of the reason, the Civil War created a whole generation of ghosts that are reminders of that war's horrors. Only in remembering the past can the past be honored. Only in remembering the dead can their lives and their sacrifices be respected.

Consider the Confederate dead of the Battle of South Mountain, whose bodies were tossed unceremoniously into Daniel Wise's well. They haunted him until he saw fit to give their bodies a proper burial. There is also the spirit of Union General John Reynolds, who haunts the dreams of Joan Bennet, exhorting her to reunite him with his long-lost love. There are the sickly prisoners of Andersonville, still emaciated and in great agony, seeking release from a peculiar cruelty of war. Those fortunate enough to encounter the living spirit of the Civil War cannot help but be moved by the experience. The dramas of war resonate still.

We hope that these stories will help those unfamiliar with the war appreciate something of its impact. For Civil War buffs, perhaps these stories will provide a different and new perspective from which to view the great conflict. In the end, we hope they will move readers as they journey back through time, into a world without which modern America would not exist.

The Civil War was a necessary step toward what a nation hoped would be a greater enlightenment, but one on which it stumbled. Slavery had been outlawed, but racism survived and many states sought to restrict the new freedom of blacks. For former slaves, the struggle for equality continued in the Jim Crow South, where blacks might as well have been slaves. Denied the vote, condemned to the most menial employment and threatened by groups such the Ku Klux Klan, former slaves still found America a most inhospitable place. The Civil Rights Act of 1964 did much to redress the past, but even in the 21st century, 140 years later, the struggle continues. The Civil War and its ghosts linger in the conscience and in the landscape—reminders that people are still fighting the same fight of so long ago.

1
Forts and Battlefields

Reenactment or Reality?
CHANCELLORSVILLE, VIRGINIA

Once a month, Sandra Skoda-Whipple and her husband get together with members of a club with close to 3000 members. The year is no longer 2003. The Skodas are no longer in Salinas, California, and Sandra is no longer a healthcare worker. Instead, she becomes a wealthy Boston socialite. Meanwhile, her husband, who usually works as an assistant manager at a jewelry store, serves as a soldier in the 69th New York Infantry. Together they cross time and space to find themselves in the northeastern United States in the year 1863, when the country was, to say the least, a very different place. And therein lies the appeal.

The goal of a Civil War reenactor is, in Sandra's words, to educate "the public about our rich culture and past." A love of history and a desire to escape from an increasingly complex and complicated world drive her and her husband Dennis. Of course, it's not to say that the late 19th century was an easier time, but it may have been less complicated than the media-saturated and conflict-ridden corporate world of today. "Civil War reenacting," says Sandra, "harks back to a simpler and more romantic time. My husband and I love what we do."

Every effort is made to recreate a past faithful to the spirit and reality of the age "down to the smallest detail." During the reenactments, spectators will see entire infantries, cavalries and artilleries pound the earth, helping people remember what men and women sacrificed in battles such as Gettysburg, Chancellorsville,

Ruins of the Battle of Chancellorsville in Fredericksburg, Virginia

Fredericksburg, Antietam and Spotsylvania. Sandra and others like her bring life to the past and render history immediate and urgent. Sometimes she is ably assisted by those best able to help: Civil War soldiers who actually fought and died in the fields so many years ago. While the reenactors do their best to recreate the past, their ability to do so pales in comparison to that of those who lived through those times. Civil War battlefields are thought to be among the most hallowed and haunted places. Sandra knows this fact firsthand.

It's not that Sandra didn't believe in the paranormal. While growing up, she saw her mother demonstrate what Sandra believed to be psychic abilities. As an adult, Sandra had seen and heard other things that might have inspired belief in the paranormal, but never anything as eerie or vivid as what she heard in a field in Virginia.

Sandra and her husband share a great love for and dedication to Civil War history. Dennis, in fact, has a personal connection to the conflict; he is the great-great-great-great nephew of Union brigadier general Amiel Weeks Whipple, who died after sustaining wounds at Chancellorsville. Earlier in his life, Whipple had surveyed for the railroad in the southwestern states; according to Sandra, Southern Pacific follows his route still. Sandra and Dennis' honeymoon reflected their interests and Dennis' personal connection to the war. They spent their time touring the Civil War battlefields, making their way through the sites in Maryland, Pennsylvania, the Carolinas and Virginia. In Virginia, where much of the war was waged, they found Hazel Grove at Chancellorsville. It was there that Dennis' great-great-great-great uncle was killed. He was buried three days later in Washington, D.C., with close friend Abraham Lincoln by his side.

The Battle of Chancellorsville, which took place over a week in spring 1863, is still remembered as Confederate General Robert E. Lee's greatest victory. Outflanked and outnumbered, Lee split his Army of Northern Virginia into three, resisting all attempts by Union Major General Joseph Hooker to dislodge his troops from positions in Fredericksburg and to avenge the Union's humiliating defeat at Fredericksburg in December. By May 6, Hooker and the Union army had retreated across the Rappahannock River. Whipple, charged with leading the Third Corps, had been directing batteries placed in a long and sloping meadow surrounded by forest—Hazel Grove—when he was killed. The victory spurred Lee's confidence; he now believed he could invade the north. In six weeks, the Army of Northern Virginia had crossed into Pennsylvania, where it encountered Union resistance at a little town called Gettysburg. The three-day battle that followed was the largest and bloodiest of the war.

Sandra and Dennis arrived at Chancellorsville late on an overcast day. Few people were there with them. Hurricane Isadore was moving ashore at the time. The clouds overhead were harbingers of the storm's impending arrival. Walking the field at Chancellorsville, Sandra and Dennis were overcome with a sense of awe and wonder. The old battlefield was silent except for the wind rustling through the trees; the field was almost a picture of tranquility. But the facts were sobering and inescapable.

Over 30,000 men lost their lives at Chancellorsville; 17,000 of these were Union men. Among Lee's dead was General Stonewall Jackson. So much blood had been shed that the grounds ran red. And although the land today is a verdant carpet once more, Sandra and Dennis could easily imagine a time when smoke hung thickly in the air, the screams of the wounded and dying sounded across the meadow and the crackle of gunfire and the clash of bayonets echoed and snapped. Dennis stood there in Hazel Grove, reading the plaques erected in the field, wondering where his ancestor might have been

At the site of the battle, a dedicated Civil War reenactor heard an eerie phantom bugler.

standing before his death. Sandra wandered up onto a hill, just listening and watching her husband.

As she began walking back down the hill, towards her husband, she heard the strangest thing. A seasoned reenactor, Sandra recognized the sound as belonging to a bugle.

"I was startled," Sandra says, "to hear a bugle blowing from within the grove." Sandra spun around, perhaps hoping to catch a glance of the bugle blower. But she saw nothing except Hazel Grove. The bugle call continued to sound, sweeping over the land. It faded but then returned for its encore, as if borne on the wind. Sandra, of course, couldn't help noticing that the air was still.

To Sandra's experienced ears, the bugle call was a summons to arms used during the Civil War. Which army it was meant for, she couldn't say. North and South used the same calls. But why was there a bugle calling to arms? Two armies had once met on that field, but Union and Confederate soldiers had long ago yielded the land to history. Sandra reasoned that the bugle call must have been a paranormal echo, a lingering remnant of the Battle of Chancellorsville.

No reenactors were at Chancellorsville that day. The worsening weather kept many people away from the site. The bugle call had come from within the grove.

"It's thickly wooded," Sandra says, "with closely bunched bushes of poison ivy. I don't think someone would have ventured into the trees to blow a bugle. Also, I would have heard laughter or talking." Sandra continued to describe how the bugle call hadn't come from one stationary source. To her, it sounded as if someone riding a horse had ridden by her and blown the bugle. One moment the sound was there, but then it faded away.

"It was a sound from the past," Sandra reasons. "That sound did not come from a real person."

Sandra didn't ask her husband about the sound, unsure of whether he might have heard it. She delayed telling Dennis about the incident, not because she thought he would be disbelieving, but because she longed to keep it to herself for a while. She had her very own, highly personalized souvenir from Chancellorsville. When she did tell Dennis, he was more than supportive.

While some may not consider a bugle call at a Civil War battlefield much of a haunting, for Sandra the incident has become an experience she will never forget. Even in a life in which she has had numerous other paranormal experiences, Sandra was still surprised and awed when she heard the soldier calling his men to arms on the deserted fields of Chancellorsville. For a passionate and dedicated Civil War reenactor, hearing a phantom bugle call might be a sublime and perfect experience—proof of the paranormal and a past that is still very much alive.

The Tunnel Hill Dead
TUNNEL HILL, GEORGIA

The lights appeared suddenly, flickering to life in the chill winter night, catching the attention of two men dressed in gray Confederate uniforms who were huddled around a sentry fire. "Do you see that?" one man hissed to the other, his voice tinged with alarm.

"What in blazes?" the other man shot back, squinting at several campfires that suddenly dotted the hillside rising ahead of them. "Who's lighting those things?"

"This don't make no sense," the first man responded. "Ain't no way that many people got up on that hill."

"Not one of those fires was there but a minute ago," came the response.

Civil War enthusiasts reenact the Battle of Missionary Ridge in Georgia.

The two men looked at each other before nodding in silent agreement. "Let's go take a look." The pair picked themselves off the ground and were just about to start for the mysterious campfires when they looked back at their rifles, which they had left in the dirt behind them.

"Maybe we ought to take 'em?"

"I think that might be best," the other man responded.

Without a word, the two reclaimed their weapons and headed out, walking carefully around the sleeping forms of their fellow Confederates, towards the small cluster of campfires scattered across the wooded hill. A fierce wind suddenly picked up, and the quiet nightscape was transformed into a blustering cacophony of swaying trees and bushes. Shuddering in the chill, the men continued towards the fires on the hill. They chose one of the fires and approached it as stealthily as they could, creeping up behind trees and bushes until they were only a few yards away.

The fire burned fitfully in a tiny clearing, buffeted by the harsh winds that were blowing harder than ever. They couldn't see anyone around it. "What is going on here?" one of the two Confederate interlopers whispered to the other. "Who lit this damn thing?"

Both men were crouched low to the ground, neither of them too eager to approach the deserted fire. "Maybe we should go take a look?"

But the moment the suggestion was made, two hands emerged from the darkness just beyond the flame, and then they spotted two boots on either side of the fire's small circle of light. The man sitting there was obviously trying to warm himself, clasping, unclasping and rubbing his hands together over the fire. The interloping pair stared at the man for a few more minutes when they noticed that gold brocade wound up his gray sleeves. He was a Confederate officer.

"He's one of ours," one man whispered. The other man nodded, indicating he had seen the color of the officer's sleeve. Yet the knowledge that this man was on their side did little to ease their trepidation. They were still frozen with fear, each of them silently convinced that something about the scene before them wasn't quite right. And then they saw his face.

He leaned forward, and his head was illuminated by the fire's orange glow. The man's face was pale as bone, without the slightest tinge of color. Even his eyes, staring into the flame in morose contemplation, were somehow colorless. He looked more like a painting of a man than a living, breathing being. The pigment of his skin looked as if it was colored by a macabre artist obsessed with bone whites, dull grays and sickly yellows.

He sat in silence, looking into the fire for a few seconds. Then, ever so slowly, his eyes moved up to the two men who were staring at him. Both lay paralyzed under the inhuman gaze, unable to move though every muscle in their bodies urged them to get up and run. The staring match continued for a few breathless moments until the Confederate officer and the fire he was sitting beside vanished right in front of them.

That was when the pair decided they had had enough. They bolted to their feet and ran off as fast as their legs would take them, not stopping until they reached their own campfires. Hunched over in breathless exhaustion, the pair did not say anything to each other, but cast their wary eyes back at the direction they had come from. Not a single fire lit the hill behind them. One man looked at the other with a look of complete disbelief on his face. "I can't believe it," he finally managed to gasp. "Did you see that? It was a ghost—a ghost of a real Civil War officer."

The two men weren't sure whether to be thrilled or terrified. They were, after all, Civil War reenactors camped overnight on Tunnel Hill, Georgia, with the intent of reliving the Battle of Missionary Ridge the next day.

The most ardent kind of Civil War enthusiasts that one might find, these men were dressed in full Confederate regalia. They camped in tents almost identical to the ones used by soldiers over a century ago, and even put themselves through infamous Civil War meals—wolfing down hardtack and quaffing muddy make-do coffee. All this to get as close as they could to those men who arranged themselves in columns and rows and marched out to face death so many years ago.

On this November night, the two reenactors came closer to reality than they ever could have expected. They haven't been the only ones. Over the years, scores of Civil War reenactors have had all sorts of experiences with bizarre phenomena on the old Georgia battlefield. The site of General Patrick Cleburne's courageous stand against General William Sherman's vastly superior forces on November 24 and 25, Tunnel Hill is one of the lesser-known Civil War battlefields in Georgia. It was there, along the northernmost reaches of Missionary Ridge, that Cleburne confirmed his battlefield brilliance, breaking Sherman's assault on the Confederate positions (although he was outnumbered nearly four to one). In the end, however, Cleburne's incredible stand was in vain, as the Confederate line broke farther south along Missionary Ridge. By the evening of November 25, the Confederates were retreating in defeat.

Yet the battle did not mark the end of the drama on Tunnel Hill. The site has become a favorite for Civil War reenactors, drawing over a thousand participants once a year to relive the battle. While the reenactments are always a grand spectacle, the spate of strange occurrences that are annually reported when the small army swarms into the region reminds spectators and reenactors alike that they aren't the only ones reliving the past. The phantom fires on Tunnel Hill are the most widely witnessed

General Patrick Cleburne showed his brilliant battle strategy at Tunnel Hill, although Confederate forces were eventually forced to retreat.

phenomena, but there have been plenty of other bizarre events that defy rational explanation.

Some reenactors claim that a horrid stench of decay will suddenly waft over parts of the battlefield during the evening hours. The smell is said to be so bad that many of those experiencing it find themselves overwhelmed by nausea. Some come very close to passing out, and more than one witness has vomited. Although the smell lasts only a few seconds, dissipating into the Georgia night before too long, those who have gotten a whiff of it are never able to forget. They are convinced that the offensive and pervasive scent is nothing less than the odor of death.

Other events, not nearly so offensive but no less alarming, have been reported by other reenactors. More than one unwitting Civil War enthusiast has been left standing numb with fear after greeting a fellow reenactor, then watching his deathly compatriot vanish before his very eyes. This phenomenon happens just enough to color the yearly meetings at Tunnel Hill in surreal shades, as the living and the dead not only walk among each other, but dress in the same uniforms and relive the same event.

So it seems that the ghosts of Tunnel Hill, just like the modern day reenactors, are incapable or unwilling to forget the bloody sacrifice that was made on the verdant Georgian landscape so many years ago. And just like the reenactors, the continuing presence of the Civil War dead ensures that some part of American society will not forget the numerous sacrifices of Tunnel Hill.

Death on the Mountain
SOUTH MOUNTAIN, MARYLAND

The dread in the air was palpable on South Mountain early on the morning of September 14, 1862. Old Daniel Wise saw it in the eyes of the thousand-some North Carolina Confederates who worked frantically all over his farm. They set up firing lines, dug in behind the stone wall that marked the borders of his land and carefully placed their cannons to cover the Old Sharpsburg Road where it approached the Fox's Gap mountain pass. Within an hour, Daniel's once-tranquil farm was unfamiliar to the old man's eyes. Rows of cabbage and corn vanished without a trace, trampled under the Confederate brigade and replaced by artillery batteries and walls of rifles bristling with bayonets. Every rifle was cocked and loaded, pointing southeast across Fox's Gap towards the approaching enemy.

Not one of the soldiers said a word to Daniel Wise while they transformed his farm into a military fortress, and Wise knew better than to get in their way. Only after every fighting man was in his proper place did the commanding Confederate officer approach the overwhelmed farmer. The officer, a young man with perfectly kept dark hair and a goatee that hung past his collar, wore a gray military coat studded with two rows of brass buttons. Gold brocade wound up his sleeves and shone in the morning sun. "Good morning to you, sir," the officer said, speaking in an ebullient Virginia accent. "I am General Samuel Garland, an officer of the Confederate

States of America. My brigade has been ordered to defend this pass through the mountain against the approaching enemy, and will do so at any hazard. Let me assure you that you will be reimbursed for any damage to your farm."

"Damage to my farm?" Wise mumbled as he surveyed the trampled mess that used to be his harvest.

"In the meantime," Garland continued, "I suggest you and your family leave this area as quickly as possible, for there are two brigades of bluecoats coming up the Old Sharpsburg Road, and we do not intend to let them pass without a fight."

The old farmer didn't need a second warning. Gathering his daughter and son and what personal possessions he could fit into his wagon, Wise left his small wooden cabin behind him. He could hear the opening shots of the battle as the first Union soldiers cresting the ridge of South Mountain found themselves facing General Garland's brigade.

The fight for Fox's Gap began at about nine o'clock in the morning. It was one desperate engagement in the larger battle of South Mountain, in which General Lee's Confederate rearguard engaged the vastly larger Union forces under General McClellan. History would remember the fight only as a lead-in to the horrific battle of Antietam, occurring three days later just beyond the South Mountain range. But for thousands of Union and Confederate soldiers, the fight for passage through the South Mountain gaps was the end of the road. Bullets and cannonballs flew back and forth, decimating Union and Confederate lines. The relentless Union advance on

General Garland's position led to fierce hand-to-hand fighting along Daniel Wise's old stone wall. Men lunged at each other with bayonets, knives and fists. General Garland himself was shot off his horse, breathing his last as his demoralized brigade finally broke out into a headlong retreat from the larger Union force.

The battle for Fox's Gap was a short affair, lasting only about two hours, but it was no less bloody for its brevity. By the time the Federals occupied the pass, hundreds of dead bodies lay thick over Wise's fields. The mountain pass was turned into a landscape of death, with soldiers shot, stabbed or blown to pieces by artillery. Union soldiers were the ones standing wearily over the battlefield after the smoke had cleared, but an onerous duty came along with victory. For though the field was theirs, so too were the fallen that covered it, and the task of burying the dead fell on their shoulders. It was hard, ugly work, made worse by the rocky ground at Fox's Gap that made the digging especially difficult. Eventually, the Union men, demoralized, disgusted and exhausted by their nightmarish detail, decided they had had enough. Eager to finish their burial detail, they gathered the last 58 Confederate bodies and threw them into Daniel Wise's well. After they were done their grisly work, the Union soldiers finally moved on. A few days later, on September 18, Daniel Wise and his two children returned home.

The Wise family couldn't have dreamed up a more horrific sight. The fertile fields they once knew were now unrecognizable, made into a surreal harvest of devastation by the numberless Union burial mounds in Wise's fields. Dead Confederates were buried in shallow trenches that were dug right up against the bullet-riddled walls of the Wise farmhouse. Death hung over the entire area, and there was no escaping the stench of rot, which was just as thick outside Daniel Wise's cabin as it was within. But the worst of it lay at the bottom of the Wise well, where 58 dead Southerners lay decomposing in the festering darkness of the dank pit.

The Civil War continued on its bloody course, leaving Daniel Wise and his ruined farm to be forgotten in the backwaters of Maryland's local history. Yet Daniel's tale did not end there. In fact, it had just begun. As outraged as he was at the mess the Union army left behind, Wise quickly learned that some of the dead on his farm were as unhappy with their burial arrangements as he was.

According to popular account, Daniel Wise's first run-in with one of the Fox's Gap ghosts occurred a few days after he returned. Wise was sitting on the porch of his home, smoking a pipe and trying to figure out what he was going to do about his farm, when a solitary young man appeared in the distance, walking down the Old Sharpsburg Road towards his home. As Wise watched the man approach, he felt a dull chill creep up his back. He wasn't sure why, but the sight of this man filled him with a strange sense of dread. Only when the stranger drew closer did Wise begin to get an idea of what sort of thing he was facing. At about 20 yards, Wise couldn't help noticing the bone white pallor of the man's skin; a few yards closer and Wise could make out the eerily blank expression on his face. When the pale man stepped onto Wise's front yard, the Maryland farmer realized that he could see right through his visitor. The man before him was transparent.

Daniel Wise nearly fell out of his rocking chair in fright. "Wh-wh-who are you?" he stammered, not sure whether he should have asked *what* instead of *who*.

The visitor did not respond, and a terrifying silence settled over Wise's yard. When the transparent apparition finally did speak, its voice sounded cold and empty, like the frigid fall wind blowing over South Mountain. "Our lives were stripped from us and we were not even given a proper burial. Be sure that I will return here every night until we are honored as fallen soldiers." The apparition then slowly turned until it was looking at Daniel Wise's well, standing for a minute or two as it grew evermore transparent, until there was nothing there at all.

Frantic and terrified, Wise ran towards the well, somehow hoping to speak with the dead young Confederate, perhaps to tell him that he wasn't the one who had thrown the men in the well, that he was just as upset about how the dead soldiers had been treated. The blood-red sun was just about to dip under South Mountain when he reached the well, and the old man frantically threw the cover back.

Leaning forward into the black pit, Daniel was just about to holler his plea when the smell of putrefaction hit him. He barely managed a tortured gag before he crumbled to his knees, his body unable to take in the poisonous stench of rot. He heard them then, as he was hunched against the well wall, coughing and spitting. Their moans rose out of the depths of the well, a tortured chorus of hopelessness and misery. The sound was so horrific that Daniel was never able to forget it for as long as he lived.

But at that moment, all he could think of doing was closing up the well and getting as far away from it as he could. Struggling to his feet, Daniel Wise pushed the lid back over the well opening and staggered back to his cabin as fast as his shaky legs could take him. Once inside, he slammed the door shut behind him, barring the entrance with a chair jammed under the doorknob. He didn't sleep a wink that night, his thoughts plagued by the appearance of the dead Confederate and the voices in the well.

Daniel Wise never went near the well again, but the dead soldier's apparition appeared on the Old Sharpsburg Road every night, just as the sun was setting. If Daniel was outside, finishing up his daily chores or relaxing with a pipe on his front porch, the ghost turned off onto his yard and made his way towards Wise. There the dead soldier stood for several minutes, staring blankly at the Maryland farmer before gradually fading into nothingness. On those nights when Daniel was indoors at sunset, the ghost went only as far as the gates, stopping there to stare at the Wise home with the same expressionless gaze until fading out of sight.

For his part, Daniel Wise never got used to the ghost's regular appearances. Every day, he felt anxiety creeping in as the sun dipped close to the South Mountain ridge and the sky began to grow dark. Sometimes he tried to ignore the apparition, moving indoors at the first sign of dusk and drawing his shutters tight. But Wise quickly learned these measures were pointless, for even when he couldn't see the dead Confederate, he could still *sense* him—standing silently just outside his fence, looking at the shuttered window of his home with blank accusation. Wise knew he was out there. Gaping in fearful silence at the walls of his home, imagining the ghost standing alone on his doorstep, the old farmer found no respite locked indoors. Somehow, imagining the presence of the lone phantom was just as frightening as standing in front of it.

The Southern casualties at South Mountain turned life on the Wise farm bad. Cursed by the daily visits of the dead soldier, Daniel did everything he could to get the Confederates in the well a proper burial. He wrote letters to Washington, complaining bitterly about the mess the Union army left behind all over his land and the well that was choked with corpses. Days turned into months, months turned into years. Although Daniel Wise kept up a constant stream of correspondence, he did not hear anything back from the federal government.

Never once did he mention the ghost in any of his missives, but word of the supernatural soldier on the Old Sharpsburg Road spread through the county. More than one curiosity seeker staking out the road at sunset claimed to see him as he drifted towards Daniel's farm. Even after 1865, when North and South settled into their uneasy peace, locals still claimed to see the ghost of the anonymous soldier making his way down Fox's Gap towards Daniel Wise's farm.

The ghost continued its vigil throughout the 1860s, just as Wise continued his correspondence with Washington, demanding that something be done about the bodies. He finally received an answer in 1874. Twelve years after the last shot was fired at Fox's Gap, the United States military sent in an army detail to clean up Wise's farm. They removed the bodies from his well and exhumed the men buried on his land for proper interment.

Daniel never saw the soldier again, and for the rest of his years he was content in knowing that his efforts granted the Confederate dead their final rest. His story, however, lived on. After Daniel Wise passed away, the tale of the ghostly soldier became a local legend. Wise's house was eventually flattened, his farm abandoned and his well buried. But the burial and reburial of the Confederate casualties at Fox's Gap is still noted as one of the Civil War's more grisly footnotes, and the tale of the old farmer and his nightly visitor remains, although it has been over a century since any phantom footsteps made their way down the Old Sharpsburg Road.

Fort Monroe
HAMPTON, VIRGINIA

Given its history, it isn't surprising that Fort Monroe, the largest stone fort ever built in the United States, boasts a varied and eclectic collection of ghosts. Among its more famous paranormal residents are the spirits of two presidents who fought for a nation and one writer whose words still strike terror in the hearts of those who read them. Abraham Lincoln, Jefferson Davis and Edgar Allan Poe are all believed to appear within the fort's weathered walls. There are a host of other spirits whose names are not as famous, but whose stories are just as fascinating.

Officers and ladies pose on the porch of a garrison house at Fort Monroe.

Fort Monroe's history begins with its geography. As early as 1609, when Fort Algernourne stood on the site, colonists and settlers recognized its importance in regulating traffic through Chesapeake Bay and the James River. Fort Algernourne was destroyed three years later by fire. In 1632, Point Comfort was built, only to be lost in an ocean storm in 1667. Old Point Comfort was erected in 1727, but was swept up and destroyed by a hurricane in

1749. Whatever fort stood at the river mouth played a crucial role in the British defense of their early colonies against Spain and colonizing nations. Of course, it wasn't long before it was the British themselves who were threatening their former possessions in the New World.

During the War of 1812, British ships sailed into Chesapeake Bay in August 1814 and sailed up the Patuxent River to launch attacks upon Baltimore and Washington. In a costly and humiliating error, the Americans had failed to realize how vulnerable their capital was to attack. Even when British troops were seen approaching the city, the city remained calm and unsuspecting. Washington was sacked, its buildings burned. Among the charred ruins were the remains of the President's Palace. As the capital smoldered, America's leaders realized that a series of forts along the Chesapeake Bay would be necessary to guarantee the future defense of their capital and other cities. It had been a harsh lesson, but one that the United States took to heart.

Planners returned to Old Point Comfort and saw that its geography gave the United States control over the mouth of the James River. A fort there would be key to defending Richmond from attack. Construction of a fort on a 63-acre site began in 1819 and was completed in 1834. The country christened the great stone structure Fort Monroe, in honor of its fifth president, James Monroe.

It was here that a young Edgar Allan Poe was assigned in 1828, only to leave three months later when he decided that the army wasn't quite the right place for him. Robert E. Lee arrived in 1831 as an engineer charged with overlooking the fort's outworks and approaches. Three close friends stationed with him were Joseph E. Johnson, Benjamin Hager and James Barnes. All became Civil War generals, and, ironically, the fort to which Lee had given his efforts remained in Union hands through the Civil War.

Fort Monroe was a rarity in the Civil War—a Union fort located in the South. But its proximity to naval bases in Norfolk was not enough to prevent the ironclad *Merrimack* from thwarting Union attempts to gain control of the peninsula. To do so, Union army planners knew that they had to bring Norfolk to its knees so that the Union army could send reinforcements to General McClellan in his campaign against Richmond.

President Abraham Lincoln arrived at Fort Monroe in May 1862 to plan the attack. It was launched on May 8, but repelled. Success was achieved a day later when Union troops landed at Ocean View. On May 10, Norfolk surrendered and, lest their dreaded weapon be used against them, the Confederate army destroyed the *Merrimack*.

It seems only fitting that at the war's conclusion, Jefferson Davis, captured while trying to flee to Texas to establish a new Confederate government, was imprisoned at Fort Monroe in May 1865. For four and a half months, Davis was kept in an improvised cell and at the mercy of his Union captors, who resented the man for leading the secessionists and for his alleged role in Lincoln's assassination on April 14, 1865. For the entire time that he was in captivity, Davis was kept in shackles, given little sustenance and treated little better than a caged animal. He was moved from Fort Monroe soon after. Only the impassioned intervention of his wife and the financial contributions of Horace Greeley, Commodore Vanderbilt and others towards his $100,000 bail bond won the former rebel president's freedom.

Fort Monroe, then, was the setting for great drama and trauma, both private and public. It was doubtless a place of great emotion and tension, and, as a result, managed to capture something of the essence of those who passed through, bearing more than the weight of all the world upon their shoulders.

Edgar Allan Poe, the conflicted author of such classics as "The Fall of the House of Usher" and "The Masque of the Red Death," wrote "The Cask of Amontillado" while at the fort. It was a story inspired by an allegedly true tale he had heard of a Virginia military man who was walled up alive in a building. One imagines the young writer, at odds with the army and his family, his head full of ideas and heart bursting with the desire to create, finding affinity with the story. Perhaps he felt all too like the man walled up in the building—trapped in stone, with no certainty but death—as he wrote in the dank and dark confines of the fort with nothing but candlelight as his companion. His ghost is believed to walk the passageways of Fort Monroe, his brow furrowed in thought.

President Abraham Lincoln, who also haunts the White House, sits at a desk in Fort Monroe, probably in Quarters No. 1 where he is believed to have stayed. Written on his face is worry, and few can even begin to imagine the agony that painted his face so. One who can, Jefferson Davis, the yang to Lincoln's yin, is seen shackled, still in his cell. At other times, in a situation that must have been the only glimmer of light during his dark days

The ghosts of Fort Monroe include Edgar Allan Poe, who wrote "The Cask of Amontillado" while stationed there.

at Fort Monroe, he is seen curled up on the floor with his head cradled in the lap of his wife. Beaten and ailing, Davis is comforted by the gentle touch of the woman, whose own face is the physical embodiment of devastation and despair.

Misery seems to be a prerequisite for the ghosts of Fort Monroe. The lesser-known spirits of the storied fort have that in common with their more famous brethren.

Within Fort Monroe is a stretch of land known as Ghost Alley. One of its residents is known only as the woman in white. It's believed that she married a captain during the Civil War. Few saw the match as amorous. At nearly twice her age, the captain had very little in common with his wife; at times, the gap in years seemed too large to span. Matters were complicated further by his duties, which often left the captain's wife alone and unloved in the confines of Fort Monroe.

Her life was beginning to feel inert, as dull and lifeless as the stones that made up the walls of her home. So, when she met a dashing young captain who took more interest in her than her husband ever had, she swooned and felt the first stirrings of what she knew was love. She expressed her emotions to the young captain, who reciprocated. Her husband returned to find the two together in his bed. While he didn't love his wife, the old man recognized betrayal and felt its sting. He brandished his weapon and the lover fled. Standing at the foot of their bed, the captain fired one shot into his wife's heart. Her last thoughts were of her lover and their love. Now she walks Ghost Alley, luminous in a white dress, forever seeking her beloved captain.

Others visiting Ghost Alley are advised not to leave roses in one officer's quarters. The history of this haunting has been lost, but whoever still roams these quarters is said to harbor an intense dislike for the flowers. Roses left in the room overnight are always found the following

The ghost in one of the officers' quarters is known for his intense dislike of roses.

morning strewn all over the floor. Why? No one seems to know.

What is certain is that Fort Monroe occupies a prominent place in American military history. The building is the third oldest active military installation in the United States, serving now as the Army's Training and Doctrine Command with a workforce of about 3100, including 1900 civilians. It has stood for over a century and a half.

But even though the facility has been updated to keep current, it is as much a living museum as it is a fort, a place where history looms large and where the past comes to life, resurrected by those who have yet to find peace in the afterlife.

Fort Clinch
AMELIA ISLAND, FLORIDA

People looking for something to do in northern Florida, besides enjoying the sun and surf, often head to historic Amelia Island. As the self-proclaimed birthplace of the modern shrimping industry and a former colony of France, Spain and England, Amelia Island is a unique place indeed. Once the playground of wealthy New Yorkers with their winter homes, the island has given way to tourists, conventioneers and history buffs. Tourists come for the resorts, conventioneers for the hotels and history buffs for a remarkably well-preserved fort.

The fort lies at the northern end of the island, occupying over 1000 acres of land and over 8400 feet of shoreline. Originally it was built to control the entrance to St. Mary's River and Cumberland Sound, by keeping unwanted visitors out. Policies are different now, and as a state park, Fort Clinch courts visitors actively with the promise of either learning what life might have been like as a soldier in the late 19th century or watching real people from the period going about their daily business. How is that seemingly impossible task accomplished? For

*The ghosts of Florida's Fort Clinch appear among visitors and histori-
cal reenactors.*

the most part, historical reenactors at Fort Clinch help to
recreate the timely atmosphere. But besides being a well-
preserved historical relic, Fort Clinch also boasts an
equally well-preserved collection of ghostly spirits.

Not surprisingly, the fort is old. Its site has been used
for various defense structures since at least 1736. The current fort was built in 1847 and named after General
Duncan Lamont Clinch, a prominent figure in the Second

Seminole War. At the onset of the Civil War, Confederate troops took control of the fort. General Robert E. Lee visited the fort twice before ordering the withdrawal of Confederate forces in 1862. After that time, the 1st New York Volunteer Engineers of the Union Army occupied the fort. Shortly after the war's conclusion, the fort ceased to operate, except for a brief period during the Spanish-American War. In 1935, the state of Florida bought the fort with an eye to establishing one of its first state parks. Three years later, the park was opened to the public, and it wasn't long before people eager to relive the past began arriving at Fort Clinch. Soon enough, employees and tourists realized that there was something unusual about the place, that spirits of those long dead still walked the grounds.

It's these spirits that keep families such as the Schmitts (names have been changed in this account) returning again and again to the fort. They came first because they wanted to do something as a family that was a little different and unusual. Living in Fernandina Beach, they could enjoy the ocean and beach anytime. But touring the fort on nearby Amelia Island by torchlight was something else entirely.

Every summer, the fort conducts tours on Fridays and Saturdays. Groups are led by guides clad in the uniforms of the 1st New York Volunteer Engineers. The guides educate the visitors about every aspect of a soldier's life in 1864, right down to their diction. So that the mood is not disturbed, guests are not allowed to use any sort of artificial light. The tour is conducted under torchlight and flash photography is not permitted.

For the Schmitt family, their first trip in 1999 was a memorable experience. Under a moonlit sky, Doug,

Shirley and their 12-year-old daughter, Celia, followed the guide around the lantern-lit fort and took in all the guide had to say. Their long and flickering shadows in the firelight only added to the atmosphere. Celia was sufficiently cowed by the dark and gloomy recesses of the fort and was actually relieved that her hopes of seeing a ghost hadn't been met.

But as time went on and Celia aged, she began hoping more and more to witness the paranormal. The more the family went on these candlelight tours, the more frustrated she became. She'd heard enough of the ghost stories, heard enough about the troop of four Union soldiers who walk the grounds, the woman in white looking for her baby, the ghostly nurse in white carrying a lantern. For a child who'd grown up in the age of sensationalism and celebrity, the eerie shadows and the gloom of the tours were no longer enough to sustain her voracious appetite for entertainment. Still, she returned faithfully every summer with her family with the hopes of seeing something spectacular. Last year, she got her wish.

"It was a dark night," recalls Doug of that tour. "There was no moon and even with the lanterns and the torches, you could still barely see 2 feet in front of you."

"Genuinely creepy," Shirley adds with a laugh. "Celia was certainly thrilled. Me, less so." Shirley apparently had every reason to think that the fort was creepier than usual.

The tour seemed as if it would begin and end as it always did, until the group began walking across the parade ground beneath the buildings, lit feebly with candles. In the near darkness of the night, the buildings were almost indistinguishable from the night sky; candles looked as if they were floating on air.

"It's like something out of *Harry Potter*," Celia whispered excitedly as she looked around her. Her parents smiled. Just then, Celia grabbed her mother's arm and tugged on it. Annoyed, Shirley stared at her daughter. Celia then directed her parents' attention to one of the buildings in the distance.

"Look, Mom. Dad. Look...what is that?" Celia asked.

The family stared at the officers' quarters. In the third window on the left, they were stunned to see a figure. What was shocking about this figure was how well illuminated he or she or it was in the near darkness of the night. The figure was glowing, lit from within like a lantern or some oversized firefly. The Schmitts didn't know what to make of the apparition, and they stood there, dumbfounded and as still as statues. Their insides were not so still. The glow dimmed and the figure now looked as if he (for it was clear now that it was a he) was being lit up with a hidden spotlight. To their eyes, the man was wearing the uniform of the Union army. He must have served with the 1st New York. Having taken the tour more than once, the Schmitts knew at least that much. Of course what they didn't know was whether they were victims of a group hallucination or had seen an actual ghost.

The soldier seemed to hear their discussion with one another. He looked at the Schmitts, smiled, nodded and then doffed his cap. When he returned the cap to his head, the darkness swallowed him up. The soldier was gone.

The Schmitts finally exhaled. They looked from the window to each other and back to the window.

"We had no idea what had just happened," Doug explains. "You hear all these stories. You're aware of [the ghosts], and then suddenly you see one and you have no idea what to think."

What the Schmitts did instead was to find one of the guides and ask him about what they had seen.

"We just wanted to know that what we'd seen was real," says Shirley. "To hear that maybe somebody else had the same sort of experience."

They weren't disappointed. The guide they tracked down explained that what they had seen, while uncommon, wasn't unusual. Indeed, after talking with some other people who were on the tour with them, the Schmitts found that they hadn't been alone in what they'd witnessed. At least three of four other families confided to the Schmitts that they had seen the same glowing Union soldier. The guide then asked them all if the ghost had appeared in the third window from the left. They nodded. The guide smiled and nodded in return.

"He told us that a soldier always appears in that window," Celia says, "and that people were always asking him about it."

Of course it's not just the visitors who see spirits at Fort Clinch. Whenever Civil War battles are reenacted at the fort, participants are required to spend entire weekends there. One reenactor is said to have woken up when he heard someone in boots approaching his bed. Yet when he rolled over to see who might be standing over him, he saw no one there at all.

A couple of volunteers saw a troop of four Union soldiers walking across the parade ground and up a ramp.

They might have thought that the soldiers were just part of the reenactment, but when the soldiers disappeared into a wall, the pair knew that they had just seen something extraordinary. The following year, when the pair returned to the fort to perform in another reenactment, they kept their eyes open for the return of the ghostly quartet. Only three returned, but it seems as if the missing soldier had a good excuse for not being there.

When the volunteer saw the Union ghosts approach and asked one of the ghosts why there were only three when there had previously been four, one of the ghosts is reported to have replied, "He's sick. He couldn't make it." Perhaps the soldier was out seeking medical aid from the ghost nurse who walks the grounds of Fort Clinch with a lantern in hand.

Celia hasn't been as fortunate as these reenactors. The spirit she saw just waved at her. When asked if she ever had a chance to see the ghostly foursome of Union soldiers, she answered excitedly, "What? Really? Someone actually talked with them? I've got to go back soon."

Here's hoping that Celia has better luck the next time she ventures out to Fort Clinch. While her parents seem to feel that seeing the lone Union soldier was enough, Celia's appetite has been whetted, not satisfied. She will definitely return to Fort Clinch, a beautifully preserved building, and steep herself once again in its magic.

Spirits of Chickamauga
NEAR CHICKAMAUGA, GEORGIA

"I still don't know what to make of what I saw at Chickamauga," says an anonymous contact we shall call John Dunn. "I've always appreciated the fresh perspective I've gotten on different Civil War battles after visiting the grounds where they took place, but in all my life, in all the battlefields I've traveled to, I've never seen anything like what came out of the woods at Chickamauga."

Like so many American history buffs, John says that the Civil War captured his imagination at an early age, when he was captivated by the drama of martial heroism that occurred on the battlefields. His appreciation of Civil War history grew more sophisticated as he grew older. But while he eventually came to immerse himself in every aspect of the Civil War, from battlefield tactics to the political causes and effects of the struggle, John had never even considered the vast number of ghost stories rooted in the historic conflict.

"I don't know. I'd never been one to think about that sort of thing," John says today. "It wasn't so much that I didn't or wasn't willing to believe in ghosts. It's just that I never really gave life, death or the afterlife that much thought." John pauses for a moment before continuing. "I admit, it sounds strange to me now, that I could have spent so much time studying the details of America's worst war without really thinking about death. I mean, of course I acknowledged the horrible human cost of the Civil War, but I never really tried to imagine what the

*Chickamauga and Chattanooga National Military Park in
northwestern Georgia*

war's casualties *meant*. Maybe I just always counted myself
among the living, and left it at that."

John's view of the Civil War changed dramatically after
his visit to Georgia's Chickamauga and Chattanooga
National Military Park in the summer of 1999. "Of course
I'd heard some of the stories about the ghosts of
Chickamauga before I made the trip," John says, "but like
I said, I never really paid much attention to ghost stories."

The stories that John refers to are the well-documented sights and sounds reported in the woods and hills of Chickamauga ever since the two-day battle reached its bloody conclusion on September 20, 1863.

Earlier the same year, Union General William Rosecrans outmaneuvered Southern General Braxton Bragg, forcing him to withdraw his army from the town of Chattanooga on July 4. Unwilling to concede the loss of the town, Bragg rallied his troops in the nearby town of LaFayette. He launched two attacks on Rosecrans' forces that summer, but it wasn't until late September that he played the gambit that led to the bloodbath at Chickamauga. The frightful battle pitted the United States' Army of the Cumberland against the Confederate Army of Tennessee. On September 19 and 20, General Braxton Bragg set his rebels loose on the Union lines, aiming to shatter Rosecrans' position and reoccupy Chattanooga. The heavily wooded battlefield limited visibility, and the fighting at Chickamauga was at close quarters, more than once breaking out into vicious hand-to-hand combat. Finally, on September 20, Southern General James Longstreet broke through a gap in Rosecrans' line and sealed a victory for the Confederates.

But at what cost? The Battle of Chickamauga turned out to be the bloodiest two days of the Civil War, resulting in nearly 35,000 casualties—16,000 Union men and over 18,000 Confederates. After the last gun was silenced on the evening of September 20, 1863, scores of local women crept onto the darkened battlefield with lanterns in their hands, searching for the faces of loved ones among the dead and dying. There was no shortage of heartache on the field that night as women recognized husbands, sons and fathers among the writhing mess of humanity that littered the forest floor. Their wails were heard late into the night, drifting through the woods and over the surrounding hills. The horrible cries chilled the blood of more soldiers than the roar of cannons ever could.

According to legend, the death and misery left an indelible impression on the fields around Chickamauga Creek. Soon after the Civil War ended, locals began talking of chilling sounds in the night—of wailing women whose bloodcurdling shrieks and heartbroken moans were heard for miles around. Eyewitnesses claimed to see solitary lights bobbing in the woods, making their way to some unknown destination before vanishing in the darkness. Some witnesses have tried to follow these lights, and a few get close enough to make out a dim silhouette next to the moving orb. Yet before anyone gets too close, the black forms vanish, leaving frightened witnesses alone in the darkness.

In darkness, perhaps, but not in silence. Accounts of strange sounds at Chickamauga are legion. Over the years, countless visitors have claimed to hear the clamor of combat on and around the battlefield. The din of this supernatural engagement is predominantly heard at night, when the distant roar of cannons intermingles with rifle fire, the clash of saber and bayonet and vague cries of men in distress. Like so many other haunted battlefields where such phenomena are reported, the sounds are said to originate from very far and very near at the same time. The faint decibel levels suggest great distance, but the anxiety of who have heard the battle is dramatic, as though the battle was raging all around.

The Battle of Chickamauga was one of the bloodiest of the war—a fact reflected in the presence of "Old Green Eyes," a disembodied head.

Yet while such phenomena have caused consternation among eyewitnesses, the most famous haunting in Chickamauga doesn't involve the sounds of a phantom battle, mysterious lanterns or mourning wails. For of all the inexplicable things that are said to occur on the old Civil War battlefield, one infamous specter has appeared so often, with such regularity, that folklore chroniclers have given it a name.

"Old Green Eyes" has been terrifying visitors to Chickamauga for over a century, appearing in the near-darkness of the Georgia twilight, a disembodied head hovering about six feet off the ground, with two enormous green eyes that burn with a phosphorescent glow. It is impossible to say how many people have laid eyes on this horrifying apparition since it was first spotted (soon after the Civil War ended), but it has materialized often enough to become one of Georgia's most famous spirits.

This was what John Dunn saw coming out of the woods when he visited Chickamauga in the summer of 1999. "It wasn't quite dark yet," Dunn recalls, "but it was definitely getting there. I had spent the entire day walking around in the battlefield, and was heading back to my car when I heard this long, drawn-out groan coming from the woods to my right."

Instantly assuming that someone was hurt and in need of help, Dunn dashed into the bush, ignoring the fearful sensation creeping up his back. "Well, I barely got three steps when this floating head burst out of the trees." Dunn says. "Imagine how you would react to something like that. I pretty well jumped clean out of my boots. I mean, this thing wasn't scary; it was *terrifying*. I can't recall exactly how I reacted. I know I yelled something and then I just turned around and ran. And I mean I ran. I ran and kept running until I reached my car and sped out of there as fast as I could go. I didn't even think about looking back until I was well out of there."

As traumatic as the encounter was, Dunn has done his best to incorporate it into his personal vision of the Civil War. "Yeah, I was scared," Dunn says, "but in a way, I'm glad I had a run-in with Old Green Eyes. It changed the way I look at the Civil War. Ever since my encounter at Chickamauga, I can't help but think about the human cost of the war. The casualty figures aren't just numbers anymore, they're men's lives—lives of men who didn't want to die. Hundreds of thousands of men, each with their own stories. For many of them, I guess they aren't over yet."

It seems not. There are a few theories about Old Green Eyes. Some claim that he isn't a Civil War soldier at all, but a vengeful Indian spirit that predated the Battle of Chickamauga. Other raconteurs add fangs, fur and a body to the usually bodiless apparition, and claim that it is the South's version of Bigfoot. But the dominant theory is that the floating head is an angry Civil War soldier whose body was blown to pieces by a cannonball, leaving nothing but his intact head lying near a mangled body. This version of the story has Old Green Eyes wandering Chickamauga, looking for the body that was pulverized during the battle. The fact that he still haunts the battlefield to this day, over 100 years after the fact, speaks volumes about the futility of his search.

Dunn tries to put it in perspective. "Everybody knows that thousands of men died during the war, but not everyone acknowledges all the ghosts left behind. I've been doing some research about ghosts in the different Civil War battlefields, and I'm just amazed at how many soldier ghosts people see across the country. I'm convinced now that many are still fighting the Civil War, every day, every night."

2
Haunted Houses

The Griffon House
NEW ORLEANS, LOUISIANA

The guards at the Griffon House had never seen a pair of more patriotic soldiers. The two men had been imprisoned in the stately New Orleans home for nearly a week. From the moment they arrived, they did not let up on the military songs, bellowing jingoistic Union army tunes at the top of their lungs, their voices carrying from the top floor to the basement and to the pedestrians down the block. One of their favorites was "John Brown's Body." They stayed up late every night, hollering the "Glory Glory Hallelujahs" of the chorus with such zeal that they quickly won the hearts of the men who guarded them. Their sympathetic captors, ashamed that two such upstanding soldiers were held under lock and key, started sneaking whiskey to their two jailed comrades. The strains of "John Brown's Body" were soon infused with drunken enthusiasm.

It was early May 1862, and the Union army under General Benjamin Butler had just occupied New Orleans. General Butler put the city under heavy martial law, imposing a harsh and uncompromising order over the city. The reviled bluecoats were stationed on practically every street corner, glowering in the hot southern sun, waiting for an excuse to throw someone in the stockades. The occupation would be remembered as one of the darker periods in New Orleans' history, in which injustice abounded and the city's prisons were filled to bursting.

Upon occupying New Orleans, Union General Benjamin Butler imposed martial law, resulting in one of the city's darkest chapters.

A good number of prominent houses, including the Griffon House, were converted into prisons to accommodate the sudden swell of convicts. The Griffon House was owned by a New Orleans socialite named Adam Griffon, who fled the city just as General Butler's troops were marching in. His luxurious mansion was promptly turned into a stockade by the occupying army, and the two men locked up in the attic were among the first to be held there.

They were in for looting, arrested just after Butler had passed his severe ordinance against theft while he was in power. Their detainment seemed especially tragic to the guards in the Griffon House. For while they may have been guilty of theft, the pair's boisterous display of northern gallantry, sung out loud all hours of the day, made them ideal fighting men for the Union cause. Or so they thought. In actuality, the prisoners' show of patriotism was a show of deception.

The two men imprisoned on the top floor of Griffon House were actually Confederate soldiers who deserted after the fighting at Fort Jackson in late April. They had been making their way through New Orleans disguised as Union officers when they were apprehended for stealing from a local merchant. Terrified that they might be found out as Confederate deserters—or even worse, mistaken for Confederate spies—the pair made sure to put on such a show of northern bravado that there would be no doubt of their allegiance.

If the two deserters were encouraged by the success of their deception, they were soon wallowing in the futility of it when they learned that Butler ordered any man caught looting to be shot, regardless of what side he was on, Union or Confederate. Suddenly the pair's charade was rendered pointless, and the two Southerners became obsessed with the idea of their imminent execution. It seems, however, that their execution wasn't imminent enough.

The city of New Orleans was still in turmoil in the wake of the takeover, and the Union soldiers were too occupied with other matters to put two petty criminals to death. Far from being elated at being granted this extra time, the Confederates-in-disguise greeted each new day with more dread than the day before, unable to bear the thought of waiting another day for their inevitable end. Finally they decided to take matters in their own hands. They bribed one of their guards to sneak two pistols into their cell. One night, about a week after they were arrested, the two men lay side by side on one of the beds. They pressed the barrels of one another's guns to the other's heart and, at the count of three, shot each other at the same time. Both died instantly.

The gruesome scene that greeted the guards the next morning made the two dead captives into celebrity casualties of General Butler, and it wasn't long before their true identities were found out. While this intrigue only added to the two dead men's popularity, it wasn't their tragic end alone that made the story of the double suicide in the Griffon House into one of New Orleans' most lasting Civil War legends.

Things would never be the same in the Griffon House again. Anyone who spent any time in the resplendent old home after the Civil War talked about the strange things that went on in the attic. Over the years, ownership of the house changed frequently, and it was used for many different purposes. But whether it was a factory, personal residence or boarding house, the stories never varied too much.

The earliest accounts of the phenomena in the Griffon House came from frightened witnesses who heard the noises in the attic. These stories were told by the first workers who were employed at the Griffon House when it was converted into a lamp factory shortly after the War. Men and women working late into the night spoke of the creaking footsteps plodding across the attic above them, of the sound of heavy chains being dragged behind. More than one employee at the factory ventured up into the garret to see who was making the sounds, but no one ever found a soul in the attic. There was only the darkened room and a strange sense of foreboding that deterred anyone from staying there too long. It didn't stop there. Even as word spread of the footsteps in the attic, employees at the Griffon House became privy to stranger, more frightening events.

The voices began a few days after the footsteps. The first people who heard them might have assumed two drunken employees had made their way up to the top floor. Raucous laughter drifted down from the attic, along with faint strains of song. Yet anyone who went up to the attic to investigate only found the same deserted room, dark and still as a tomb. The singing continued, night after night, growing more and more pronounced, until witnesses were able to make out the words of "John Brown's Body."

By this time, most people believed the incidents on the Griffon House's top floor were linked to the two men who had killed themselves there. Not only were the disembodied voices obviously singing the same song the deserters had sung during their incarceration, but more than one pedestrian walking by the house at night claimed to see two pale men dressed in Union uniforms, silently staring out from the attic window. It is said that no one who caught sight of the ashen faces believed they were looking at living men. Some onlookers experienced a jolt of panic when their eyes took in the two men at the window, and they were possessed by the sudden urge to run as far away as they could. Others found themselves staring agape at the faces, overcome with a sense of terrible awe, comprehending on some level that they were witnessing some sort of manifestation of death itself—that they were staring at a reflection of the fate that awaited them all.

If the two dead soldiers in the Griffon House attic became a symbol of mortality for a small number of New Orleans residents, the persistent sightings of the ghosts over succeeding generations also made them into one of the Crescent City's most enduring legends. Indeed, given the accounts of people's experiences in the Griffon House over the years, it seems as if the spirits there have grown more active, and more famous, with each passing decade. While early reports were limited to the sounds of song, chains and footsteps from within, and sightings of the two through the attic window from the outside, later stories were far more chilling.

The Griffon House continued to be used as a factory through much of the early 1900s, and the people who had most of the run-ins with the house's spirits were employees working the late shift. The employees had largely gotten used to the occasional singing and stomping around in the attic, learning to accept the supernatural phenomena with a surprising nonchalance. And then the ghosts changed their habits.

It began when the footsteps moved to the stairs. They were big, unnatural footfalls that boomed through the house with every step, as if some giant of a man was lumbering down the stairs. The footsteps never made it to the base of the stairs, always stopping just before reaching the last step. Yet the moment the sound of the thunderous descent abated, the chorus of "John Brown's Body" was struck up by the phantom voices that were so often heard in the attic. This time, however, the drunken pair seemed to be much closer, their disharmonious singing loud and clear, as if they were standing right next to startled witnesses.

Soon after they ventured down the stairs, the spirits took up the habit of tossing things around. More than one late-night worker stared in horrified fascination as a chair suddenly flew across a room, as if hurled by some angry invisible force. Sometimes this force acted with incredible strength, tearing fixtures from walls and hurtling them great distances down Griffon's halls. On occasion, this phenomenon has resulted in near fatal consequences, as some objects have just narrowly missed witnesses, who have had to dodge out of the way of a flying table, chair or chandelier.

Indeed, there is evidence that the ghostly pair have become more angry with the passing years. Even as some people in the Griffon House were being attacked by flying objects, others began to talk of sudden temperature drops in the house, causing individuals to shiver in the middle of sweltering New Orleans summers. There were other accounts of invisible hands that would sporadically grab and shove people as they walked through the home.

The most famous incident that was said to have occurred in the Griffon House took place sometime in the

1950s, when the old home was converted into a boarding house. An elderly female resident was woken from a nap by the feeling of something dripping on her forearm. She opened her eyes in groggy curiosity and was instantly startled awake at the sight of her bleeding arm. Assuming that she was cut, the woman wiped the blood off her skin to get a better look at the wound. But her skin was unmarked; there was no trace of a gash. She was staring in confusion at the smear of blood when another drop fell onto her arm. That was when she looked up.

In the next moment, she ran screaming from her room, garbling in near unintelligible panic about the "bleeding house." The landlord was in her room investigating within the hour. Sure enough, when he looked up, he saw the same thing that sent his tenant running in terror. A section of the ceiling was a saturated smear of blood, which fell, one drop at a time, right next to the woman's armchair. The room was right underneath the attic.

Assuming that something or someone was bleeding on the top floor, the landlord dashed upstairs, only to discover a completely deserted attic. There was no trace of a bleeding carcass, and the thick layer of dust on the floor suggested that no one had been in the room for quite some time. The old woman's suite was cleaned up, but the story of the bleeding ceiling quickly spread, and the landlord soon had to lock the room up for lack of any tenants desperate enough to stay under the now-infamous attic.

By the early 1980s, the years had caught up to Adam Griffon's old house on Constance Street. Once stately, the home had become an abandoned and dilapidated shell in one of New Orleans' less distinguished neighborhoods.

While very few stories about the Griffin House circulated during this time, among all the crumbling homes on the block it was the only one that the city's destitute didn't use for shelter. It wasn't any harder to get into than the other houses, but there were whispers about all the strange sights and sounds coming from the house. Occasional passersby claimed to see the faces of the two soldiers in the attic window. Others were said to hear the faint strains of song from within. And then there were those who only looked at the house and sensed that there was something very wrong—something that no length of time will ever make right.

The Battle of Franklin
FRANKLIN, TENNESSEE

Allie Pierce hadn't always lived in Franklin, Tennessee. She moved to the city in 1997, just as she was set to start the eighth grade. It would be another year before she heard the stories about Carnton Mansion—tales with which the children of Franklin had been regaled for generations. When she heard the stories, they resonated with her and it didn't take long for Allie to embrace Franklin lore.

Franklin is a small community, with a population of just over 40,000, but its size belies its place and prominence in Civil War history. The Battle of Franklin is often referred to as the "Gettysburg of the West," a catastrophic defeat for the Confederacy that effectively crippled

Nearly 9000 men perished in the pivotal Battle of Franklin, often dubbed the "Gettysburg of the West."

the Army of Tennessee. While there were other bloodier battles, such as Antietam and Gettysburg, the Battle of Franklin is cited most often not only for its casualties, but also for its savagery and brutality. More men from the Army of Tennessee were killed in the five-hour battle than in the two-day Battle of Shiloh and the three-day Battle of Stones River.

The Battle of Franklin was a portrait of humanity at its worst and most desperate, remembered as the bloodiest hours of the Civil War and witnessed by the families of Franklin as men fought and died in their yards and fields. Among the witnesses were the McGavocks, who saw their plantation home transformed into a field hospital and morgue. To be sure, they lived the rest of their lives never having forgotten what they saw there that day. They now haunt the land, revenant reminders of a past that can never be forgotten.

Determined to prevent Union General William Sherman from reaching Savannah, Georgia, and razing it to the ground like Atlanta before it, Confederate General John Hood launched his Tennessee Campaign in 1864. He moved through Georgia, Alabama and into Tennessee, intent on preventing the 4th Corps from reaching Nashville and joining up with the rest of the Army of the Cumberland. If Hood could destroy all that remained of the Army of the Cumberland, then he could draw Sherman into a fight.

Hood's plan was to intercept the 4th Corps under Major General John M. Schofield's command at the Duck River crossings. The plan failed, forcing Hood to try the tactic again at Spring Hill. Hood realized that the isolated 4th Corps could be overwhelmed. Unfortunately, by the time the two sides had engaged each other, night was falling, bringing a halt to the skirmishes. By day's end, the Confederates had failed to dislodge the Union troops. Hood decided to resume the attack in the morning. He could not have known it then, but he was letting his best opportunity to defeat the Union army slip through his fingers. Under cover of darkness, Schofield and his men abandoned their positions and raced towards a town 12 miles north: Franklin.

When Hood realized what had happened, he marched his men in rapid pursuit of the Union army. Schofield, meanwhile, set about establishing defenses and positions on the southern edge of town. He realized the necessity of both when he learned that the men would have to stop to repair Franklin's bridges in order to transport the supply trains. By late afternoon, Hood's army of over 25,000 had arrived. Their footsteps pounded the ground, throwing up clouds of dirt and dust and rumbling across the fields like low thunder. Despite protests from other officers who claimed that the Union army was too well fortified, Hood ordered a frontal assault on the Union positions. The move was suicide. The men knew it. The officers knew it. Hood knew it too, but he charged confidently and his men did the same.

On a battlefield just two miles long and one-and-a-half miles wide, the two armies fought and fought closely. Guns and rifles were used as clubs, and cannon fire rained upon the field. Men used everything at their disposal and they fought blindly, concerned only for their own survival in a field obscured with smoke. By the time night brought the conflict to an end, close to 9000 men lay dead or dying. Over two-thirds of them belonged to the Confederacy, and six were Confederate generals.

Many of the wounded struggled for life in the rooms and halls of Carnton Mansion. The beautiful home, the centerpiece of a lush and vast plantation, had served as the family home of the McGavocks since the early 19th century. It now served as a field hospital, populated by those who, before the war, could only have dreamed of setting foot in such splendor and luxury. A soldier described the scene, writing that "the wounded, in hundreds, were brought to the house...and all the night after…when the noble old house could hold no more, the yard was appropriated until the wounded and dead filled that…"

Conditions were less than ideal. The countless number of field amputations that doctors were forced to perform resulted in a grotesque pile of limbs that reached up to the second floor of the mansion. Shorthanded, the doctors needed all the help Carrie McGavock could spare as she rushed from one room to another. She held the hands of men who wanted nothing more than to see their families one last time and whose eyes betrayed their fear and absence of hope. She pressed dressings into wounds that seemed impossibly large, craters of flesh and blood, and then watched helplessly as the men expired. The bodies were carried away, placed atop sickening piles of the dead that stood four feet high. And still the wounded kept coming.

The dead Confederates were buried in shallow graves days later. Following the war, in 1866, the McGavocks were appalled when they realized how horrible the burial conditions were. Bodies were being exposed to the elements as the wind bore away the soil under which they lay. The McGavocks decided to designate two acres of their land as a cemetery. Almost 1500 men were re-interred in the McGavock Confederate Cemetery so that they could finally rest in peace. Yet, even still, eternal rest proved elusive, as Allie Pierce, like others before her, would discover.

She had heard the stories, heard about how Carrie McGavock can still be seen roaming through Carnton Mansion, her skirt still red and soaking with the blood of the dead. Friends also told her about the ghost of

Confederate General Patrick Cleburne, whose footsteps can be heard rumbling across the porch and around the yard. Allie didn't quite know what to make of all the stories she heard, but she was definitely curious to see for herself if they were true.

Carnton Mansion is now a museum run by the Carnton Society. It is open to the public and visitors can enter the house as well as the cemetery. Allie went to the house one day with a friend and was awed by the home's beauty. Like many others, she found the beauty of the house and its manicured grounds jarring; having heard the stories of bloodshed and death, she had somehow expected something else entirely. Green fields, scattered with hay barrels, and lush gardens, verdant with a stunning array of plants, surrounded the Greek Revival home. It was idyllic. Allie and her friend didn't stay long, deciding instead to return at night.

That night, with darkness upon the land, the mansion looked quite different. The winding road became mysterious, only hinting at what might be lurking within the shadows. A thick fog had rolled in, and Allie could barely see in front of the car. The fog dissipated, eerily, just as they drove around the bend leading up to the Carnton Mansion gates. There the car stopped, just outside the gates. Ahead of them was nothing but darkness. Allie peered into the pitch and noticed that the fog was beginning to envelop the car.

"Hey, are we going to go?" she asked her friend, excitement creeping into her voice.

"Uh…" her friend started hesitantly, "maybe we should go get some other people. For our safety, you know."

Her friend drove off. But instead of collecting other people, he dropped Allie off at her home, saying that he had something to do and that he would return some other time.

"He was such a chicken," Allie says. "I was completely bummed because he chickened out."

Not to be deterred, Allie returned just days later. This time, she abandoned her fearful friend and recruited her closest and best friends: Taylor, Brittany and Myrandah. Eager for adventure, they got into Taylor's Jeep and set off for the mansion, priming themselves for the experience by retelling the creepy and eerie accounts they'd all heard throughout the years. By the time they arrived at the gates, the girls were thoroughly spooked. They held each other tightly, almost afraid to breathe. Allie felt as if a "bunch of eyes" were watching her.

Their original plan was to drive up to the mansion and take some pictures. Plans, however, have a way of changing. As they drove through the gates, fog rose up to greet them. The Jeep turned a corner, and there, bathed in the stark shadows thrown up from the glare of the Jeep's headlights, was Carnton Mansion, squatting glumly in the night.

"Suddenly, out of the corner of my eye," Allie writes, "a figure appeared on a stack of hay."

Her friend Brittany saw the figure too and reacted with a scream. Confused and unsure of what to do, the driver, Taylor, turned sharply, realizing only at the last moment that she had moved the Jeep into the figure's direct path. She swerved again, narrowly missing the stack of hay. By then the figure had vanished. The Jeep raced across the field, which had become an obstacle course with its abundance of potholes and hay barrels.

"I looked at my screaming friends and grabbed the handle on the door even tighter," Allie writes. The Jeep flew through the gates and sped down the dirt and gravel road from which it had come. Only when they looked back and saw that the house receding into the distance did the girls feel relief.

As jarring as the experience was, it served not to dull, but to whet Allie's appetite for the paranormal. Allie has a long history with the paranormal, having lived in several haunted houses over the years. Time has fostered and nurtured a curiosity about the ethereal world. Shortly after her first visit to Carnton Mansion, Allie returned again and again, sometime with friends who were skeptical about her claims, and at other times with friends to deposit tape recorders in the cemetery in the hopes of recording paranormal activity. On occasion, Allie will play back the tapes and hear, mixed in with the voices of other like-minded teenagers, what she considers "pretty creepy stuff."

It's been more than five years since Allie first went to Carnton Mansion. She goes to college now, away from Franklin, so she doesn't return to the haunted house as often as she would like. But every time Allie returns home, she makes a point of visiting the house with her friends. Franklin just wouldn't be Franklin without it. The ghosts have endeared themselves to Allie, and she does her best to make sure that others after her will be able to enjoy Carnton Mansion as richly and fully as she did.

While she was volunteering at the mansion, Allie and her friend Brittany were walking through the cemetery and were appalled to find that one of the graves had been desecrated. It was an insult not only to history, but also to the men and women who saw their lives changed forever on the day that the Civil War came to Franklin.

The McGavock children who died young were all buried in the family cemetery. One infant's grave was marked with a tombstone upon which was set a stone lamb. But on that day, Allie and Brittany realized that it was missing, that someone had defaced the tombstone and remove the lamb. Hoping to restore the sanctity of the baby's resting place, Allie and Brittany placed a stuffed toy lamb near the grave. The stuffed toy rested there for months before nature took its toll and it was removed before it rotted away.

Allie has no way of knowing for certain, but she's nearly positive that the spirits are happy for what she's done to restore the tombstone. She recognizes Carnton's place in Franklin history and how much the home has come to mean to her. The ghosts of the Battle of Franklin must know that their sacrifices were not in vain, and that as long as souls like Allie are around, they will be remembered.

At Home with a Ghost
MICHIGAN

When the Piehls met over a decade ago, Randy was blissfully unaware that he had a roommate in his house. Only when he invited Nancy into his home was the truth revealed about his peculiar houseguest.

"Yeah, she was the one who realized it," Randy admits.

As Nancy explains, the first time Randy invited her in, "I walked into his house. I hadn't been there for one minute and I said, 'You have a ghost in this house.'"

Randy was incredulous. He told Nancy quite simply that she was wrong. Nancy, however, would not be swayed. She might have met Randy only hours before, but Nancy had known ghosts all her life.

From the time she was a "little tiny kid," Nancy has had an uncanny ability to sense paranormal presences. All she needs to do to determine if a home is haunted is walk through its entrance and close the door. Then it begins. She feels it—the touch of a chilly breeze on the back of her neck. So cold is the breeze that the hairs on the back of her neck stand on end. And then, with its icy tendrils, the wind works its way down her spine. The sensation is particularly unique and difficult for Nancy to describe, like telling a person who has always been blind what it is to see. But while some individuals may dismiss Nancy's particular abilities and her stories, there are believers who have witnessed for themselves what Nancy can do.

Years ago, in Toledo, where Nancy was born and raised, she was looking for a room to rent. On 4th Street, she noticed a vacancy in a beautiful historic house. She knocked on the door, but there was no response. Not to be deterred, Nancy went next door, where the neighbor claimed that the house was her aunt's, and that she'd be happy to show Nancy around. When the two walked into the dining room, Nancy stopped and turned to the neighbor.

"Excuse me," Nancy started, "but did someone die in this room recently?"

The neighbor's eyes widened and she spoke slowly, as if unsure of the words that might come out of her mouth. "Yes, my aunt died in there. That was just two weeks ago." She paused, scrutinizing the stranger in her aunt's living room. "How did you know?"

"Because she's still here," Nancy answered. "Tell me. Was your aunt about 5'8"? Was she a thin lady with gray hair that she liked to tie in a bun in the back?"

The neighbor gasped. "My goodness," she exclaimed. "You're right on the money." One imagines that Randy's reaction would have been quite similar, because, as it turns out, Nancy was also right the first night they met.

His conversion was slow but steady. The more Randy listened to the house, the more he heard sounds that he just couldn't explain. At first, he tried to blame the disturbances on Nancy's many cats. But Nancy defended her pets, always pointing out that her cats couldn't be the culprits because they were all outside the house.

"In our office area," Randy says, "we've got shelves that have some paint cans on them. At night, at around two in the morning, you could hear someone playing them like they were drums. Not real fast, but real slow." When Randy and Nancy got out of bed to see what was going on, they found that all the paint can lids had come loose; the sound they heard must have been the popping of the lids.

Soon after, objects from around the house began to go missing. It didn't seem to matter what they were, if they were left out in the open, away they went.

"You might lay something somewhere," Randy explains, "and you knew you doggone well laid it there and it wouldn't be there the next day." One day, it might have been Nancy's earrings. The next, it would be Randy's tools. Thorough and exhaustive searches of the house would turn up nothing, and the Piehls would forget about the "little things" and move on. But the objects had a way of reappearing as suddenly and inexplicably as they had disappeared. Months would pass, and suddenly Nancy would find her missing earring in her jewelry box, right where it should be. Randy would find his hammer, tucked away neatly, as it should have been, inside his padlocked toolbox.

"Things would just reappear," Nancy says. "Right under your nose."

Randy knew that he could no longer blame the disturbances on the cats, but his rational mind still yearned for more definitive proof than his wife's instincts. He would soon have it.

First came the chills. On a hot, breezeless day, Randy would be sitting in a chair when he'd find himself shivering because of a chill that passed through his body without warning. Moments later, he would be sweltering in the heat again. He was puzzled as to why his house seemed riddled with these random cold spots, but he was beginning to ask himself whether the sudden and inexplicable chills might be the calling card of paranormal spirits. Reality finally and fully set in the day Randy was sitting on a couch in his living room.

"I caught a glimpse of something going through the air," Randy explains. "It was like a shadow or an object. I looked real hard again, but there wasn't anything there. Now I see the shadow all the time."

Often, at night, he'll see the figure and, unable to sleep, he'll wake Nancy up to point at the shadow walking up the stairs. Both have seen the figure many times now, and Randy even claims to have seen it walk through a wall. They even have a photograph of the apparition, which appears in a picture as a white mist. Nancy is certain that the photograph is positive proof of the ghost; it is the second of two consecutive pictures that she took of her husband. The first is mist-free.

Aware now of the spirit in his home, Randy had no idea what might happen next. Should he be scared? Would the ghost try to harm them? For answers, he turned to Nancy, who, up to that point, had had them all.

"You do not have to fear the dead," she told him. "Fear the living—they're the ones who can kill you." Nancy further explained that this particular spirit was far from malicious, saying that she felt he was a "friendly guy, maybe a bit of a nuisance who just wants to assert himself." To do so, he'll take items and return them later, and he'll appear to Randy on those many sleepless nights. And just a couple of weeks ago, Nancy was sitting at her kitchen table, smoking. She had placed her lighter and cigarettes on the table when suddenly the lighter leapt up off the table and fell to the floor with a clatter.

"It was as if someone had picked it off the table," Nancy says, "and then just dropped it." Nancy, exasperated, told the spirit to go somewhere else and picked up the lighter.

When asked who the spirit might be, Nancy offers a puzzling answer. When she sees the spirit, one assumes in the same manner that she saw the dead aunt, what she sees is a young man dressed in the gray uniform of the Confederate army. His face is ashen, a study in sadness etched with wrinkles and eyes that gaze longingly out at something beyond. One must wonder, of course, how a Confederate soldier came to haunt a home in southern Michigan.

After all, Civil War battles were never fought on Michigan soil, and the state was staunchly abolitionist. Many young men from Michigan did fight in the war, but they fought for the Union. Even so, Nancy still feels that the ghost is definitely a Confederate soldier. Census records from the late 19th century do indicate that almost 200 Confederate soldiers had settled in Michigan. Perhaps Nancy and Randy's ghost was among them. The house in which they live was probably built in 1900, and while she and her husband have added another floor, the ghost is only seen in the older parts of the home.

Is he here for a reason? Nancy believes that the soldier might be. According to her, the ghost might still be trying to communicate with her. What Nancy has found interesting is that ever since she moved in with her husband, they have received peculiar phone calls.

Either one of them will answer, but there will be no response on the other end. It could certainly be a prank caller, but the calls have been happening now for over 11 years, and either the Piehls have themselves an extraordinarily patient prankster or perhaps someone is calling from beyond the grave. After all, the phone calls happen almost every day, always around 6 PM. Everything they've done to find an answer has only clouded the mystery further.

Dialing *69 to determine the last number that called reveals nothing. The Piehls' call display indicates "Unknown Number." They went to the phone company and the police and had them tap the phone line, and even then they still had nothing. The phone company said that they couldn't even see that calls had been made to the line. It was as if nobody was calling. The Piehls have changed their phone number twice and the phone still rings. Nancy is convinced that someone from beyond is trying to contact her. She heard that these phantom phone calls are typical of "someone who has passed over and might be trying to communicate with you." The phone calls still occur, but Nancy is now waiting for some sort of clue as to what to do next.

"I'm sure he's trying to communicate with me, but most times I'm too stupid to figure it out or too lazy to bother," she says. Fortunately, the ghost seems to have reserves and reserves of patience. Of course, that isn't surprising. He has, after all, been dead for years and seems content to wait a little longer.

And while Nancy is certain the soldier means her loved ones no harm, both she and Randy suspect that there may be a spirit within the home that might be more menacing.

The presence of another spirit would be odd, since Nancy cannot sense it. But in 1996, something inexplicable and strange happened to her favorite cat, Dolly.

Nancy has always believed that animals are far more sensitive to spirits than humans. So she wasn't completely surprised when her cat seemed to be reacting to a person or thing that wasn't there, but she was perplexed and frightened at the change that overcame Dolly.

Randy and Nancy were sitting on a couch in their living room when Dolly walked into the room and just stopped. She just sat and stared at the ceiling for an hour while Randy and Nancy exchanged puzzled glances. What Nancy was certain of was that her cat was terrified.

"She was scared out of her fur," Nancy says. "Her every hair was standing on end and I was convinced she was going to have a heart attack. After that night, she wasn't the same for two years. Nobody could get close to her except me." What confuses Nancy is that none of her other many pets reacted or were affected in any way.

"I've never seen a cat with such big eyes," Randy adds. "She was scared stiff." And then, four years ago, the cat reverted back to her old self, allowing Randy to approach and play with her. In fact, Nancy complains that Randy has become Dolly's favorite.

"Oh, she hangs on him something terrible," she says, laughing. "Animals have a sixth sense. They know when you're sick and you need attention." Randy has been sick for a while now and spends most of his time in hospitals. "The cat…just loves him to death," she says, "just like me."

Of course, Nancy still wonders what scared Dolly so much. It couldn't have been the Confederate soldier. His is a friendly spirit that had never bothered the cat before. The identity of whatever frightened Dolly continues to remain a mystery, and it seems as if it will stay that way.

As for the Confederate soldier, his activity has decreased since Randy and Nancy have adjusted to his presence. They believe he has calmed down now that they know and accept him. Indeed, Randy has become comfortable enough with the spirit that he has taken to telling several people about their special houseguest. When they stare at him incredulously and ask him how he could stand to live in such a house, the one-time disbeliever just laughs and says, "The ghost is harmless."

"He really is harmless," Nancy affirms. "He really is a part of the family. It's almost like we can't do without him."

The Confederate Officer
PENNSYLVANIA

Growing up, Donna Floyd never believed in ghosts or spirits. Her father had told her ghost stories when she was a child getting ready for sleep, but she thought he was just trying to entertain her. Over the years, Donna has become more open to the idea of the paranormal, but she still isn't too sure that ghosts exist. A recent visit to her parents' house might have changed her mind.

Donna had recently returned from a trip to Europe; it'd been months since she had seen her family, so before returning to her home in Indiana, she stopped in Pennsylvania to see her parents. They were happy to see her, and were always happier when her old bedroom was no longer empty. After all, Donna had grown up in the house, spending 15 of her 25 years in the small bedroom at the top of the stairs, just off to the right. As soon as she was settled in, her parents called her downstairs to the den. They wanted to hear all about her trip and see all her photos.

She showed them her photos of Rome's Trevi Fountain, of Gaudi's buildings in Barcelona, and the crisp and impossible blues of the Mediterranean from Greek beaches. She raved about Versailles in Paris, Buckingham Palace in London and Holyrood Palace in Edinburgh. And then she laughed as she recounted the haunted tours of castles that she had taken, how she had found them alternately amusing and frightening, how she had screamed when someone had accidentally brushed against her arm in a particularly dark hallway.

Donna's father, Dan, laughed. He recalled how, as a child and even now as an adult, Donna hated hearing stories or watching movies that had anything to do with the paranormal. She was easily scared and the idea of ghosts and goblins was more than enough to terrify her. The fact that she had gone on a ghost tour was surprising, and he thought to himself that maybe now she'd be ready to hear his stories.

"What stories?" Donna asked.

Her father began to tell Donna that their house was haunted and always had been. Donna was incredulous. How could that be, she thought to herself. She had grown up in the house from the time she was two until she left to study at Indiana University at 17. Through those 15 years, she never saw anything that would have led her to believe that their home was haunted. Her childhood, in fact, was rather dull and uneventful. Not that there was anything fundamentally wrong with that, but Donna remembered wishing for some sort of excitement. Maybe ghosts would have been the ticket. How odd, then, for Donna to hear that while she might have lived in the same house as her father, they had had wildly varying experiences in the home.

"Mom," she said, turning to face her mother, who sat quietly stirring cream into her coffee, "did you know this too?"

Donna's mother, Debbie, smiled. She said that she'd been told a while before about their paranormal guests but that, like her daughter, she'd never seen anything out of the ordinary.

"But I still believe, Donna," she said, casting her eyes towards her husband. "Because he believes. And because there will always be things in this world that resist comprehension. You and I—we just don't have the sensitivity that your father does." Donna stared peculiarly at her mother and then at her father. She motioned for him to continue and elaborate.

He told Donna how he had experienced strange things in the home from almost the first moment that they moved in. Dan couldn't explain it, but he always felt sudden chills that were inexplicable. He would be watching television in the den, snuggled warmly beneath his flannel blanket and in his reclining chair, when the air would turn cold. Looking around, he couldn't see that any windows or doors were open to admit a draft, and besides, it was only fall. The chill he felt reminded him not of red and orange leaves but of frostbitten toes and numb fingers, of winter at its coldest and harshest. He would pull the blanket tighter around his body, covering his freezing nose with its edge. Moments later, Dan would be sweltering. The chill had passed as suddenly as it had come. As something he couldn't quite explain, he just ignored the phenomenon. Soon enough, he became accustomed to the strange freezes and barely even noticed them when they occurred.

He never mentioned the strange phenomenon to Debbie, but asked her every now and then whether she had noticed any odd drafts in the old house. She hadn't, but she did point out to Dan that the house was very old and there were probably some drafty areas in the place. After all, they were living in a home that had stood for years. She guessed that it might have been built not long after the end of the Civil War. It was only natural that such an old home would have its own quirks and tics. Doors squeaked, the floorboards creaked. So what if the house had cold spots too? Dan knew there was more to the cold spots, but he just didn't know where to begin looking for an explanation for them. He did ask around quietly and discovered that previous owners had talked about the cold spots, saying that they meant that spirits were near.

Spirits? Dan was certainly intrigued now. Oddly, though, while previous homeowners mentioned having seen the ghost of a man, Dan had yet to see anything of the sort. He found himself hoping to catch a glimpse of something—maybe mist or a shadow. He confided his hopes in Debbie, but told her to keep the possibility that their house might be haunted a secret from little Donna.

Did a Confederate officer materialize before several members of a Pennsylvania family?

She was a skittish child, easily rattled and, when scared, prone to have crying fits that might last well into the evening. Debbie understood and joined her husband in his vigil. Dan didn't have to wait long.

Dan had turned part of the garage into a workshop and spent a couple hours each day there, tinkering with an assortment of projects, most associated with restoring and renovating parts of the old house. One evening, he had finished priming a door and decided to stop for the day. Under a starlit sky, he walked back to the house. He paused to look up at the sky. How insignificant was he compared to the size and age of the universe, he thought.

Shaking his head, he looked back down and stepped back in complete shock. There, standing before him, was an old man. He had clear blue eyes, a cloud of puffy white hair and a beard. He wore a rumpled suit that looked eerily similar to those Dan had seen in the Civil War museums scattered throughout the northeast. It was a little tattered and looked as if it had seen more than its fair share of action, but the resemblance was undeniable. The translucent figure before him was wearing the grays of the Confederate army.

He stood there, his eyes fixed on a point somewhere beyond Dan. In his mouth was a pipe from which smoke rose. Two things about the smoke struck Dan as extremely odd. It was a breezeless night, yet the smoke drifted lazily to the right as if caressed by a wind. And while there was much smoke, Dan couldn't smell the tobacco. It was apparently odorless and immune to the laws of physics. Surely this was the man that previous homeowners had mentioned. Dan now had his evidence of the paranormal and knew that the cold spots signaled the presence of the old Confederate soldier. He watched, trying to keep his tongue from lolling out of his mouth as the wizened soldier smiled at him and then disappeared into the night, leaving Dan to wonder whether the whole thing had happened or if he had just dreamed it all up.

He rushed to tell Debbie what had happened, and she listened, entranced and flabbergasted. She cursed herself, wishing that she had seen the apparition along with her husband. Privately, she swore that she would see it next, but, alas, the soldier never appeared to Debbie. Perhaps he didn't like women. After all, while the Floyd women never saw the Confederate soldier, Dan's brothers all witnessed the phenomenon for themselves.

During a family barbecue, Dan's two brothers were relaxing in the backyard, savoring the ribs Dan had expertly grilled and the salad Debbie had made. While the men sat and smoked cigarettes, Donna and Debbie worked at washing the dishes. It was then that the Confederate soldier decided to appear to Dan's brothers.

Dan had gone into the woodshed, leaving his brothers and an empty seat behind. As the brothers talked, they saw, out of the corners of their eyes, a figure materialize in the seat that Dan had just vacated. They stopped talking. Their cigarettes fell from their lips. Both first looked at each other, then at the old man dressed in Confederate grays, and then back at each other. The soldier simply smiled, took a pull on his pipe and exhaled. He took the pipe from his mouth, nodded at both brothers and then disappeared. Dan returned to see his brothers staring at his empty chair. He knew that they too had seen the ghost. He laughed and reassured his brothers that everything was fine, that the ghost was just a part of the house.

To his slightly stunned brothers, Dan explained how whenever something odd happened in the house, he and Debbie just said it was the ghost. He explained, amused, how his car keys or razors would go missing, only to reappear days later. He had seen a shadowy figure move across the den on more than one occasion and would often hear the floorboards creak in the house when he was certain that his wife and child had gone to sleep. He could see that his brothers were still slightly unsure of what to think.

"You guys really still doubt me?" he asked. "Come on. What'd you guys just see? You want to explain to me why you guys looked so terrified for a moment there? Looked ready to pass that dinner you just ate."

It was true. How could they doubt Dan when they had just seen a man appear and disappear out of and into thin air? Over coffee and after Donna had been put to sleep, Dan told Debbie what had happened.

Donna sat at her parents' kitchen table in surprise. Parts of her questioned her father's stories; after all, he might have been a great storyteller, but he'd been known in the past to exaggerate and embellish details for either comic or dramatic effect. Was he doing the same now? Donna couldn't be sure, but she was almost certain that every word her father had uttered that night had been true. She could see the conviction in his eyes, hear the integrity in his voice. And her mother, who usually chastised her husband when he distorted facts, had sat quietly next to Dan throughout the evening. She only spoke a couple of times to see if Donna had wanted more coffee.

"Well, Dad," Donna said, shaking her head. "I am glad you waited to tell me. I would have been petrified. Even now, I'm a little shaky." She showed him her hands, which were trembling slightly.

"You don't have anything to worry about sweetheart," Dan said, winking at Debbie. "Just remember to sleep with one eye open."

Donna laughed. But she remembers thinking that her father hadn't given her the same advice. The ghost hadn't appeared to any of the women in her house just yet, but who's to say when that might change? Luckily, Donna spent a night free of paranormal disorder. Or so she tries to believe. She did awaken in the middle of the night to the sounds of the creaking floorboards, but somehow she managed to convince herself that it must have been her father. She resisted the temptation to check, not wanting to know otherwise.

Not long after, she returned to her home in Indianapolis. While she never admitted it to her parents, she was glad to be back in the Hoosier State. She would certainly miss her parents, but she was sure that she would do just fine without the ghost.

"I wasn't quite ready to believe," she says. "I'm a little less skeptical. That should be enough, shouldn't it?"

McRaven House
VICKSBURG, MISSISSIPPI

When Abraham Lincoln was elected president in 1860, Mississippi acted on an official resolution that it had adopted in 1859. On January 9, 1860, Mississippi declared that it was seceding from the Union. The state loathed Lincoln the abolitionist, the man threatening their constitutionally protected rights to own slaves. Mississippi was not alone. South Carolina had seceded first, and by February, seven other states had followed suit.

In Montgomery, Alabama, representatives of the seceding states met to elect a head for the Provisional

Confederate Congress. Jefferson Davis was elected as the leader for a slave-holding South. Two days later, he delivered his first address as the president of the Confederate States of America in Vicksburg, Mississippi. It was a momentous occasion. For the first time, the Confederacy was presented as a nation united under one cause, one constitution and one man.

Vicksburg was crucial to the Confederacy's survival. The North surely would not tolerate the Southern states' secession, and war was all but assured. When war came, Vicksburg was key to controlling the Mississippi River. Founded in 1811, Vicksburg grew rapidly as a center for commerce, agriculture and river traffic. With the completion of the Vicksburg-Clinton Railroad line, the city had become the western link of the only east-west railroad between Memphis and New Orleans. Looking down upon the Mississippi from its perch high on the bluffs, Vicksburg became known as the Gibraltar of the Confederacy. So long as it still controlled the Mississippi, the South would remain whole. The North understood the river's importance and launched a campaign to wrest it from Southern hands.

By 1863, Vicksburg was the last of the great Mississippi River port cities still under Confederate control. New Orleans, Baton Rouge and Natchez had all been ground under Admiral Farragut's heel. Vicksburg was all that stood between the North and control of the Mississippi. Troops arrived at the city, and Farragut called for its immediate surrender. Vicksburg refused, and Farragut quickly understood why the city had been so bold and brazen. He could not elevate his cannons high enough to

*After a lengthy assault, General Grant's Union forces occupied
Vicksburg, Mississippi, in July 1863.*

strike Vicksburg as it sat atop the bluffs, and a direct
frontal assault would be the equivalent of mass suicide.
He returned to New Orleans, leaving in his wake a shattered Southern economy and hordes of people fleeing the
Lower Mississippi Valley.

Farragut's campaign was followed by General Ulysses
S. Grant's. By the spring of 1863, the Army of Tennessee
had marched through Louisiana and into Vicksburg on
May 22. Grant attacked the city, but his troops were

repelled, learning through experience what Farragut had suspected through instinct. He decided to suffocate the city instead, establishing a line of structures around the city and cutting Vicksburg off from supplies and outside communication. For the next 47 days, Grant barraged the city with cannon fire; soldiers and citizens suffered during the siege and many began digging caves out of the hillsides, hoping to escape the artillery fire. As supplies became meager, Vicksburg residents became desperate for food. Mules, horses, dogs and rats were all consumed without compunction. Confederate General Pemberton and his commanders knew that surrender might be a foregone conclusion.

Ironically enough, Vicksburg fell on the Fourth of July, 1863. With its defeat, the South was cleaved into two. Grant's victory, combined with Meade's bloody stand at Gettysburg, had turned the tide of the Civil War. Federal troops occupied the city and made their headquarters in McRaven House. During the siege, it had served as a field hospital.

Left in command, Colonel Wilson attempted to ease the occupation and ameliorate a city embittered with the horrors of its siege and destruction. Wilson turned to Captain McPherson, a former resident of Vicksburg, to patrol the streets of the city, giving out food and clothing to the needy so that the Union army might not be so reviled. McPherson walked the streets nightly, taking in the complaints of the people and the 30,000 paroled Confederate soldiers. One evening, however, McPherson didn't return from his tour and Wilson grew suspicious.

McPherson's worst fears were confirmed when, after weeks of fruitless searching for the captain, he was awakened by a noise while he slept. Wilson sat up in bed but saw nothing. He fell back asleep only to be reawakened again. His bed was shaking. Was there an earthquake? A tremor? The colonel leapt from the bed and looked around. He gasped as he saw standing before him a figure, soaking wet and with a beaten and mutilated face. His eyes opened wide with terror as he realized that the figure was none other than Captain McPherson.

"What happened to you?" Wilson whispered.

McPherson replied that former Confederate soldiers, a little tipsy from the drink, had fallen upon him while he was walking by the river. Inebriated, their emotions were running high and when they saw McPherson walking in his federal blues, they beat him within an inch of his life and then threw him into the Mississippi, where he died.

"Why have you returned to tell me this? Who were these soldiers? They will pay for your death with their lives," Wilson proclaimed.

McPherson then explained why he had returned, to tell Wilson that his death must go unpunished. "Only in this way," he said, "will the next generation not hate us as this one does." McPherson knew of what he spoke. Vicksburg bitterly refused to celebrate the Fourth of July for 81 years. Even today, there are pockets in the South where some believe that the war is not yet over.

Was McPherson wise in advising his colonel not to seek revenge? Who knows? One could ask his spirit, perhaps. After all, he still walks the halls of McRaven House, one of Vicksburg's most haunted homes.

Some defeated Confederates killed a Union sentry after the occupation, resulting in a celebrated haunting at McRaven House.

McRaven's tortured history has all but guaranteed its place as a home for spirits. It was built in 1797 as a family home. When it served as a field hospital during the Civil War, it saw many deaths, and it's rumored that some of these dead soldiers were buried in the yard. Lost and aimless, they wander the grounds of this historic home, occasionally frightening the unsuspecting.

Inside, there are other spirits as well. Once, in 1984, a tour guide was leading a group through the restored house. A woman in the group, taken with a beautiful piano in the parlor, asked the guide if it still worked. The guide pressed down on one of the keys, shook his head and said, "It doesn't look like it." Eerily, though, when the group left the room, they heard, coming from the parlor, the opening measures of a waltz being played on the piano.

As the years passed, owners complained that the spirits of McRaven House were becoming increasingly agitated and aggressive. Visitors to the house reported feeling overwhelmed and overcome with a wave of nausea as they stepped across the threshold. One individual had his hand almost crushed when a door slammed on it. Of course, he was alone in the house when this accident happened. Perhaps it was the same spirit who had pushed another individual to his knees while he was walking through the parlor.

Thoroughly terrified, the house's owner at the time moved out so that the spirits could be exorcised. When he returned, he knew immediately that the malicious spirits had been driven away, leaving behind only benign ones, Captain McPherson among them.

In the year 2000, McRaven's owner, Leyland French, allowed CBS News correspondent Susan Spencer to report on the home. During his interview, French revealed that the house is indeed still haunted, and that it is home not to just himself, but also more than a few ghosts. He claimed to have photographs as evidence. To draw the ghosts out, French whistles Dixie.

Others agree with French, including parapsychologists William Roll and Andrew Nichols, who toured the home in 1999 during a full moon on Memorial Day weekend and during a reenactment of the fall of Vicksburg—an appropriate time for the ghosts of McRaven House to appear.

According to Spencer, the two parapsychologists, professors at the State University of West Georgia, discovered that McRaven sat upon a powerful magnetic field. These fields are typically created by household wiring and the earth itself, but there are places where they can be especially concentrated. The higher the concentration, the higher the chance of a paranormal incident. At McRaven, according to the parapsychologists, the high magnetic field does indeed lead to paranormal incidents.

In an interview with Spencer, Nichols described McRaven House as "a kind of storage battery for these energies, and people who go into this house are exposing themselves to those energies…in that sense, McRaven House is…a genuinely haunted house." The energies in McRaven House enhance the mind's ability to perceive paranormal presences. In a way, they liberate the mind from its own inhibitions.

McRaven House is a place of opportunity, then, a place to open up the mind. In doing so, visitors will find themselves taking a rather unexpected trip. They will embark on a journey through time, to a darker time when the soul of the United States came perilously close to giving itself over to its darkest impulses. As it did on McRaven House, the war left an indelible mark on Vicksburg, which suffered, as did many other Southern cities, through the bankruptcy and internal strife of reconstruction governments. Today, Vicksburg is home to 30,000 people whose role in the Civil War is memorialized by both a national park and the ghosts of McRaven House.

The Beauregard-Keyes House
NEW ORLEANS, LOUISIANA

The violence of Civil War battles was a terrible thing to behold. Whenever North met South on battlefields across the country, the roaring machinery of death came to life with an awful force, unprecedented in the annals of military history. Cannons rained down on enemy positions over great distances. Soldiers were blown apart by 6-, 10- and 12-pound balls of lead that flew across contested territory. Rows of riflemen carried Springfield and Enfield rifles that were accurate to nearly half a mile away; their fire swept over approaching columns like an invisible scythe. While soldiers of the Civil War were subjected to all sorts of awful advances in technology, the generals continued to conduct their fights as generals had for over a century. Drawing upon Napoleonic military tactics, Civil War officers—Union and Confederate—took strategies out of books that were written when the weapons of war weren't nearly as effective.

And so it was that entire regiments of men were ordered to march across open ground, just as their predecessors who fought over Europe half a century before had, holding rigid marching formations as they were ripped apart by crashing cannon and withering rifle fire. Casualties were not only heavy but highly visible and exceedingly gruesome. Civil War battles were brazen expositions of the worst humanity was capable of, and few who looked upon them and survived would ever be the same. Yet given the brutality of this style of fighting, there has been surprisingly little written about the effects of the fighting on the minds of the men who fought.

This is surprising because we have gotten so used to hearing about the troubles that plague soldiers after they are exposed to the horrors of war. Post-Traumatic Stress Disorder was first diagnosed among veterans who were having difficulties coping with everyday life after their experiences in the jungles of Vietnam. In World War One, it was called "shell shock." Psychologically scarred World War Two veterans were said to be suffering from "combat fatigue." Yet even as society has acknowledged these casualties in every military conflict of the 20th century, very little has been said of the shell-shocked Civil War veterans. How did the men who survived the horror of a Gettysburg, an Antietam or a Shiloh cope with the world after they fulfilled their duties?

Only recently has any historical research been done on the mental trauma of Civil War veterans. The latest studies do indeed suggest that a good number of men had difficulty coming to terms with their experiences. Certainly, anybody witnessing the strange goings-on in the famous Beauregard-Keyes House in New Orleans might get the impression that at least one Civil War soldier continues to struggle with the horror of the things he had seen on the field of battle.

Pierre Gustave Toutant Beauregard was one of the premier generals of the Confederate Army. A native Louisianan who showed great promise at West Point, graduating second in his class, he rose to military prominence during the Mexican War and was appointed superintendent of West Point just months before the Civil War

The Beauregard-Keyes House in New Orleans

broke out. Beauregard was a stern and competent officer whose pride in his Southern roots equaled his military reputation, so no one was surprised when he made the decision to support the Confederate cause.

It was actually General Beauregard who was responsible for the opening shots of the Civil War, since he ordered the bombardment of Fort Sumter on April 13, 1861. The Southern papers made the acclaimed "Hero of Fort Sumter" into something of a celebrity, and a few months later, he commanded the Confederate Army of the Potomac to victory during the First Bull Run. Dubbed "Little Napoleon" by his military peers for his admiration of Napoleon Bonaparte, after Bull Run the Creole General might have dared to dream of a legacy comparable to that of his martial hero. If he did entertain any such fantasies of military glory, they were quashed in early April 1862, when Beauregard took command of the Confederate forces during the Battle of Shiloh.

The first major engagement in the Civil War's western theater, Shiloh saw the meeting of 65,000 Union soldiers with roughly 44,000 Confederates on the west bank of the Tennessee River over April 6 and 7. It was a bloody two-day seesaw of attack and counterattack, and when the smoke cleared over the contested ground, there were over 24,000 dead, wounded and missing, with the Union forces standing over the field. Beauregard's first loss was a major blow to the Confederacy. The Union victory at Shiloh led to the occupation of Corinth, Mississippi, a major railway hub for the Confederacy and a key strategic location.

By all accounts, General Beauregard had difficulty dealing with what he experienced at Shiloh. Shortly after retreating from Corinth, the "Little Napoleon" went on a sick leave for over two months, without Jefferson Davis' permission. The Confederate president was outraged at the Creole General's insubordination and ordered that Beauregard be permanently stripped of his military rank. By September of that year, a shortage of skilled officers caused Davis to rescind his order, and Beauregard was reinstated to a military command. Beauregard served the Confederate army for the duration of the Civil War but would never live up to the promise of his first months.

Retiring to civilian life after the Confederate defeat, Beauregard went on to become one of New Orleans' leading citizens, making a tidy sum in railroad development and serving a term as Louisiana's adjutant general. But despite his post-war affluence, there is reason to believe Beauregard had some difficulty leaving the war behind him—especially the Battle of Shiloh. Indeed, the strange and inexplicable experiences of many who have visited the Beauregard-Keyes House in New Orleans' French Quarter have led them to believe that what the general saw at the critical Tennessee battle left a deep and lasting mark on his psyche. Beauregard lived in the stately mansion that carried his name for only one year, from 1865 to 1866. A short time, yes, but apparently it was a time in his life that he would never forget, a time that was loaded heavily with tortured memories of the first battle the general lost.

The stories about the Beauregard-Keyes House begin in 1893, the same year the general passed away. It was in that year that people walking by Beauregard's former residence late at night first heard the voice. The voice was old and raspy, and in a tone that landed somewhere between horror and regret it spoke "Shiloh...Shiloh" over and over again.

None who heard the mournful mantra believed it came from anyone, or anything, that lived. It was distinctly unnatural, a voice barely above a whisper that somehow seemed to come from a very great distance. It was as if a man somewhere inside the darkened house, lost in a nightmare, was muttering the object of his dread over and over in a fitful sleep. And yet passersby were able to hear the terrified whispers, as if the sleeping man was lying right next to them, somehow conveying his terror on all who heard the two tortured syllables. Many who

The ghosts of Beauregard and some of his fallen soldiers relive the bloody Battle of Shiloh.

heard the name of the Civil War battle found themselves running away from the Beauregard-Keyes House as fast as their legs could carry them.

It didn't take long for people to link the whispering voice to the former resident who lost the battle and whose name was being whispered. The assumption that some postmortem remnant of General Beauregard still resided in the New Orleans mansion gained currency when house residents began to talk of a semi-transparent apparition that appeared in the ballroom in the middle of the night. According to witnesses, the shimmering figure was dressed in a Confederate gray military uniform and bore a striking resemblance to photographs of Beauregard as he appeared in the prime of his life. Most people who saw the general standing in the ballroom did not stand around gaping for too long. The sight of Beauregard was often accompanied by a severe temperature drop that chilled witnesses to the bone. Some who saw the general claimed that they were moved by an almost instinctual drive to turn around and run, sensing, on one level or another, that the figure standing in front of them was a ghostly expression of pure misery.

Luckily for those living in the Beauregard-Keyes House, the ghost of General Beauregard did not stay in the ballroom for too long. It is not known exactly when he stopped appearing, but within a year reports of run-ins with Beauregard's ghost stopped. Yet whatever relief residents of the mansion may have felt was short-lived, for soon after Beauregard's spirit ceased its loitering in the ballroom, another equally disturbing phenomenon began. That was when the general and his solitary cry for the battle he lost was replaced by a supernatural manifestation of the battle itself—when the ballroom transformed before startled witnesses' eyes into a ghostly Shiloh, complete with bugles, drums, rifles, artillery and casualties.

The cacophony of battle was heard only late in the evening, and like Beauregard's whisper it was tinged with surreal intonation, somehow sounding very far and very near at the same time. Anyone woken by the sound of battle late at night could follow the ruckus down to the ballroom, where, according to legend, they were in for quite a sight.

There, instead of the Beauregard-Keyes ballroom was a sort of phantom rendition of the Battle of Shiloh. Those who witnessed it told of rows of weary-looking men standing in a surreal landscape dotted by vague visions of trees, river and hills. Some likened the sight to an impressionist painting, others to some bizarre dreamscape they were more likely to see in their sleep. The men standing in rows—soldiers from the North and the South—did not actually fight but remained deathly still, staring ahead expressionless as the muted sound of battle boomed and cracked through the erstwhile ballroom. Long moments would pass, during which most witnesses, awestruck or frightened, believed that they were looking upon some sort of supernatural roll call. They soon realized that, one by one, the soldiers in front of them were taking injuries. It happened with every crash of cannon and fusillade of rifle fire: one member of the phantom troop would suddenly be perforated through the chest, another would lose an arm, yet another would have his leg blown off and crumple to the ground. Yet still they remained there, the dead of Shiloh, staring ahead in silence even as they were being cut down by the distant sounds of rifle and cannon.

Many who have witnessed the haunting in the ballroom turn and run before the ghostly battle has run its course, while those possessed more by curiosity than by fear stand and watch until each soldier is struck down. It is then that a speedy decomposition begins, as the visage of every fallen soldier rapidly changes into a grinning skull, and the cuts and lacerations of wounded limbs fade into clean bone. And then they are gone. The end of the supernatural scene always turns out the same, concluding the moment the morning sun rises over New Orleans. That is when the skeletal apparitions gradually fade into nothingness and the hills and trees of the ghostly Shiloh are replaced by the furnishings of the Beauregard-Keyes ballroom. By the time the sun has risen, not a trace of the supernatural battle remains.

Unlike the ghost of General Beauregard, the phantom battle has been consistently reported throughout the years. Just as subsequent owners spoke of the strange sights and sounds in the ballroom, reports of the phenomenon continued for years, even after the doors of the Beauregard-Keyes House were opened to the public, when the mansion was made into a National Historic Site. Passersby late at night will still talk about hearing sounds of battle coming from within. And despite statements by the house's caretakers that they have never seen anything out of the ordinary in the ballroom, the house curators have acknowledged that there is something about the house that frightens them. A good number of paranormal enthusiasts and investigators alike consider the house to be one of New Orleans' premier haunted sites.

It is interesting that the ghost of General Beauregard stopped appearing after so short a time, while the ghostly vision of Shiloh, his greatest defeat, continues to be reported today, over 100 years later. Could this be evidence of how deeply the Louisiana general was affected by what he experienced on the Tennessee battlefield? Perhaps Beauregard was more sensitive than history gives him credit for, and suffered greatly for the horror he saw on April 6 and 7, 1862. He lived in the Beauregard-Keyes House for only one year after the Civil War, but could it be that the memory of the battle was so intense that he could not forget it? Could he have wandered down to the ballroom in the middle of sleepless nights, where—in the same feverish delirium experienced by so many other veterans who lived through horrific battles—he relived the details of those two terrible days night after night after night? Can it be that these flashbacks were so intense that they left some sort of psychic residue in the ballroom that is still felt today? That would mean that the ghosts haunting the Beauregard-Keyes House are not the ghosts of the soldiers who died at Shiloh, but the ghosts of General Beauregard's nightmares—the remnants of one man's struggles with the horrors of the Civil War.

The Nelson House Dead
YORKTOWN, VIRGINIA

Joanne Hawthorn (a pseudonym) prefers to keep her real name to herself when discussing certain details about her recent trip to Yorktown, Virginia. "You know, I never really believed in ghosts and that sort of thing," she says. "Basically, I've always been a 'what you see is what you get' sort of person. But that was before my recent trip to Yorktown. Really, I don't know what to believe anymore, but all I can say is that I'll never forget what I saw at the Nelson House."

As the former estate of one of colonial Yorktown's leading families, the Nelson House has a history going back to the early 1700s, when an industrious merchant-planter named Thomas "Scotch Tom" Nelson commissioned its construction. The house eventually became the seat of the powerful Nelson clan, which dominated local politics during Virginia's colonial era. During the War of Independence, Scotch Tom's grandson, Thomas Nelson, Jr., was an ardent supporter of the patriot cause and spent much of the Nelson fortune backing the rebellion against the British Crown. As commander of the Virginia militia, he ordered his men to fire on the town, and home, of his birth, on October 19, 1781, when American patriots besieged General Charles Cornwallis' loyalist army, fortified in Yorktown. It was during this battle that the famous cannonball, fired during the patriot bombardment, was lodged in the brick gable of the Nelson House.

The cannonball is still visible today, protruding between two attic windows. It has become an accidental memoriam to the struggle that gave birth to the United States. Yet this isn't the only conflict that the Nelson House has seen in its long history. For Yorktown was the focus of another, far more grisly, conflict some 80 years later when the Civil War raged across the country.

General George McClellan was marching his Army of the Potomac up the Virginia Peninsula towards Richmond when he ran into General John Magruder's small force of Confederates entrenched in and around Yorktown. Although Magruder's force was vastly outnumbered, with only 13,000 fighting men to McClellan's near 90,000, Magruder's cunning deployment of his men led the cautious McClellan to believe he was actually facing a force larger than his own. The Confederates used the Nelson House as a field hospital during the ensuing siege of the Yorktown fortifications, transforming the once stately colonial abode into a nightmarish den of human suffering.

Much has been written of the brutality of Civil War medicine. There were far too many overworked, under-qualified and uninformed surgeons performing their "healing" in septic conditions so bad that almost every man treated was certain to develop a major infection of one kind or another. Most surgeons treated wounded extremities by hacking off the injured limbs, and after major engagements, field hospitals were invariably located in the middle of bleeding piles of arms and legs. Many soldiers, putting on their best show of military bravado, joked that they would rather face a row of enemy riflemen than their own surgeons. Yet no man who spent any time in a field hospital found the quip even slightly amusing.

The Confederate stand at Yorktown was only a holding action; a badly outnumbered Magruder ordered the retreat in late April, just before McClellan was about to begin his attack in earnest. The real battles of the Union's Richmond offensive occurred farther up the peninsula, where the Confederates aimed to halt McClellan's march to Richmond in a series of bloody engagements throughout the month of May. Although casualties in Yorktown were comparatively light—the Confederates lost little more than 140 men—they were still high enough to fill the Nelson House with shattered bodies.

A primitive triage was set up, where the incoming casualties were stationed in the house according to the severity of their wounds. Minor wounds were treated on the first floor, most of the grisly amputation work was done on the second and those poor souls deemed wounded beyond remedy were put in the attic. One can only imagine the horrible scene on the third floor. Overcrowded with men mangled beyond remedy, the attic was filled with the cries of mortal lamentations, as soldiers facing imminent death gave voice to insoluble regrets, shouted for absent loved ones or spent their last moments in agonized concentration, struggling to hold on to rapidly diminishing consciousness. As he lay gasping his final breaths, a soldier with enough presence of mind might have pondered his final fate. Thinking about the ultimate meaning of his sacrifice, he may have realized then, in a dreadful moment of black epiphany, that in a few years, there would not be a man, woman or child alive who would remember who he was or understand the depth of his loss.

The Nelson House was emptied after the Confederates vacated Yorktown. Drawn into the spotlight during the early phases of McClellan's Peninsula Campaign, the old Virginia town was occupied by Union forces for the rest of the war, and gradually receded into the national memory. Yet if life in Yorktown went back to relative normalcy after the Civil War, things at the Nelson House were never the same.

Very few people talked about it during the first decades following the war. The Nelson family continued to live in the house until 1907, and while some stories circulated about the house during this time, the Nelsons were very guarded about what—if anything—they saw within the four walls of their family abode. Some visitors spoke of chill drafts that suddenly blew through hallways and rooms. When they asked their hosts about the source of these drafts, they were answered only with awkward silence. There were also those guests who caught sight of darting shadows moving in the periphery of their vision—moving shapes that faded to nothing the moment startled witnesses turned to face them. And then there were the Yorktown locals who did not need to walk into the house, who spoke of the strange sense of foreboding they felt by merely looking up at the dark attic windows when they walked by.

But it was only after 1907, when the Nelsons moved out, that the historic house became widely recognized as haunted. It was said the building was plagued by the angry spirits of Confederate soldiers who died there in

April 1862. Successive owners talked about the supernatural residents that lived in the house with them and the heavy feeling of dread that hung in the dark and musty attic. Purchased by the National Park Service in 1968, the Nelson House was fully restored and made into one of the central attractions in Yorktown's Colonial National Historical Park, serving to educate and entertain Americans with their historical legacy. People have come from near and far to visit the town where the War of Independence was effectively concluded.

Yet many who visit Nelson House anticipating a piece of America's colonial past often find something very different in the old brick building—experiences far more dramatic and unsettling than they ever could have expected. Which brings us back to Joanne Hawthorn, a young woman from Richmond, Virginia.

"A girlfriend and I drove to Yorktown for the weekend, just to take a look around, really. Both of us grew up near Yorktown, but neither of us really took the time to see it. Well let me tell you, we saw a lot more than either of us bargained for."

Joanne and her friend made the trip down to the historic town on a balmy Friday morning in the summer of 1999. Arriving in Yorktown just before noon, the pair had a quick lunch and then set about taking in the local attractions. "It was a busy day, and by the time we got to the Nelson House, it was sometime past three. Well, I have to say that I got a weird feeling from the first minute I saw it. I still remember the weird chill I got when I looked up at those attic windows. I couldn't explain it, but the place just *felt* wrong."

Joanne immediately told her friend about her vague apprehension, but she received very little commiseration. "She just laughed at me," Joanne remembers, "making jokes about how the place was haunted and I was channeling the spirit of old Scotch Tom." Responding to her companion's ribbing, Joanne tried to shake off her inexplicable fear and made her way into the house.

"The feeling just kept getting worse and worse the closer we got to the house; by the time we were inside, I had goosebumps going up and down the back of my neck. That was when my girlfriend started to get a little bit creeped out too." Noticing how genuinely frightened Joanne had become, her friend began to take the situation much more seriously, and the mood between the two women suddenly became very serious. "Do you still want to be here?" Joanne asked her friend.

As anxious as the pair had become, their curiosity about the house they had just discovered overshadowed their fear. "Well, my girlfriend just looked at me and nodded. As scared as we were, the whole thing was actually quite exciting. I kept telling myself that it was broad daylight, and we were in a public building—what could possibly hurt us?" What Joanne experienced in the Nelson House that day wouldn't harm her so much as it would impel her to reconsider her ideas about the world.

The pair latched on to a group that was just starting a tour through the building. They learned then about Scotch Tom and his grandson, Thomas, Jr.—about how Yorktown was the last major battle of the War of Independence and how Cornwallis' surrender in the same town turned out to be the British Empire's admission of

The historic Nelson House in Yorktown, Virginia, is said to be haunted by Confederate soldiers who died there in April 1862.

defeat. But very little was said about the house's use during the Civil War, and when the group walked by the attic staircase, they were told that the third floor was currently off limits.

Joanne grew increasingly fascinated with the house during the course of the tour. "Something about the place just spoke to me," she says. "The history was just so interesting, but more than that, the house just seemed to be"—Joanne pauses before continuing—"alive."

"When we were told the attic was closed to tourists, I became convinced that the secret of the house, the heart of the place, was upstairs, and I just *had* to see it for myself." Joanne told her friend that she intended to get a peek of the attic, to discover whether it was closed to visitors. Her accomplice nodded with a mischievous giggle, thrilled at the idea of a little bit of adventure. The pair waited until there was no one around and dashed up the narrow stairs to the top floor as quickly and quietly as they could.

"My heart was just pounding away when we got up there. It was nothing at all like the rest of the house. It was dark and dusty and totally unkempt. But what got both of our attention right away was the smell, this disgusting musty sort of rot that I've never experienced before. At first, there was only a trace of it—just enough to make us both look at each other and sort of say 'What is that?' "

Whatever it was, it was getting stronger. A few seconds after the two women got to the attic, the pungent smell of rot was overwhelming. That was when the mood in the attic changed. "Things got really frightening then," Joanne says. "The smell got so bad that my girlfriend sort of doubled over and started to gag. It was obvious that someone, or something, wasn't happy about us being up there."

Joanne was just about to lead her friend out of the attic when she heard the first moan drift through the darkened room. "It came from one of the corners, this sad and scary groan, like there was a man there in horrible pain. I remember my first thought was that there was someone up there who needed help, and I felt an urge to run over to the corner where the voice was coming from, even though my eyes told me that there was no one there."

That's what her eyes told her, but all her other senses were telling Joanne that she was in a place of great suffering. A moment later, the first moan of pain was joined by another one, and then, a heartbeat later, yet another. Soon the room was filled with the sound of men groaning in agony. "I remember being torn between feeling really bad for the guys who were making those noises and really scared about what was going on," Joanne says. "My friend was in a lot worse shape, though. The smell in there was *really* bad, and I could tell that she needed to get out of there fast. I grabbed her hand and was just about to start leading her out when I saw him."

A dark silhouette was standing against one of the attic windows, facing the two women as they were turning to go downstairs. Joanne froze, her feet rooted to the floor in fear. "My mind was telling my legs to get moving, but I wasn't going anywhere—I didn't dare. I remember being very scared of the thing that was looking at us, like if we moved, it would lunge at us." Joanne calls the shadow "it" because the figure was shaped like a man but it was also transparent. The light from the window behind the silhouette was slightly visible, as if it was being filtered through a dark sheet. It had no physical form; Joanne was staring at a shadow without a body, an immaterial form of someone who once was. "I'm not sure how long we stood there staring at the shape," Joanne says, "but when it took a step towards us, we bolted. That was it, we had seen enough."

The pair tore down the stairs, out of the house and into the sunny Virginia afternoon, not stopping until the Nelson House was a good distance behind them. Joanne still remembers the terror of the moment all too clearly. "I can tell you, it took quite awhile for our hearts to slow down. Both of us were completely terrified, and we had no idea what to make of what just happened. I think we both assumed right off that we had just seen spirits from the Nelson House's past, but it was too much to absorb all at once, and most of the ride home to Richmond was pretty quiet. Eventually, we ended up opening up about our experience in Yorktown. Neither of us has been quite the same ever since."

Joanne ends her story there, resigning herself to a for-ever-altered view on life and death, but the ghosts of Nelson House are not lucky enough to have such a neat ending; their story goes on and on. For Joanne isn't the only person who has had a run-in with the spirits in the attic.

Over the years, numerous witnesses have heard the eerie groans coming from the top floor of the Nelson House. More than one pedestrian walking by the house at night has looked up uncomfortably at the old building's dark attic windows, overcome by the sudden feeling that something inside was watching them. Apparently, some have had far more chilling encounters. Jackie Eileen Behrend's book, *The Hauntings of Williamsburg, Yorktown and Jamestown*, includes the testimonial of Cindy Murphy. She watched in horror as the attic window slowly slid open and an angry man's heavily bleeding face emerged from within, glaring at Cindy and the four friends she was with. Having heard of the Nelson House ghosts, Cindy knew with one look at the face above her that she was staring into the eyes of a dead man.

No one can say for sure how long the Civil War wounded in the Nelson House attic will continue to relive their last tortured moments. Perhaps the despair they experienced in the former colonial home was so bad that they will remain there in perpetuity, floundering in their pain and anger for as long as the building stands. Or maybe the anguished spirits will fade over time, as the fateful 1862 spring that claimed their lives recedes further into the past.

3
Haunting Characters

Ghost of the Southern Spy
RICHMOND, VIRGINIA

Her name was Elizabeth Van Lew, but people in Richmond called her "Crazy Bet." Not that Miss Van Lew was anything short of completely sane, brilliant even, but it was just that she was in possession of a number of traits that were frowned upon in 19th-century society women. Elizabeth Van Lew was an intelligent, proud and idealistic woman who had a habit of questioning the world around her and expressing her opinions freely. Of course anyone with such a peculiar set of characteristics would have eventually run into trouble in the Old South, where an institution such as slavery was not only allowed to exist, but even considered natural.

While most of her peers were fretting over marriage prospects, gossip and the latest French fashions, Elizabeth Van Lew was stewing over the injustice of slavery. Her father, John Van Lew, might have been able to curtail her confrontational tendencies if he had nipped them in the bud. But out of his three children, Elizabeth was his favorite, and he was loath to confront her about her opinions, even though his home was staffed entirely by slaves. Indeed, John Van Lew only made things worse when he sent Elizabeth off to school in Philadelphia. The big Pennsylvania city was a hotbed of abolitionist sentiment, and there Elizabeth met a good number of like-minded individuals who hardened her convictions. By the time she finished her schooling, Elizabeth was entirely opposed to slavery. Needless to say, things got hard when she moved back to Richmond.

More than anything else, her father wanted her to find a decent man to marry and settle down with, but nothing was further from Elizabeth's mind. She was adamant about doing her part to end slavery. There were nightly rows at the Van Lew household as John tried to convince his daughter that the latest gentleman caller was just the man for her, while Elizabeth kept trying to convince her father to set their slaves free.

It turned out that father and daughter were matched when it came to stubbornness, and neither gave an inch. Elizabeth grew more and more resentful and took to making scenes when the Van Lews were entertaining guests, raving about the injustices of slave labor and often insisting that she help in serving the guests. Word got out about these public outbursts, and it wasn't long before Richmond society was snickering about the ardent young woman. They started calling her "Crazy Bet," and the stream of suitors who had come calling for Miss Van Lew's hand quickly dried up.

The prospect of spinsterhood didn't seem to bother Elizabeth, who kept vociferating for the end of slavery. Her father passed away just before the Civil War began, and the first thing she did was free every slave belonging to the Van Lew estate. She didn't stop there. Elizabeth also spent most of her inheritance buying the freedom of many of her former slaves' relatives. By the time the first shot was fired on Fort Sumter, Elizabeth was not only considered to be crazy, but she was also nearly broke.

Before her former home was demolished, the ghost of "Crazy Bet" Van Lew, a Union spy, would appear on a nearby street.

Yet she still had the Van Lew mansion and her good name, both of which she would use to good effect during Richmond's war years. Union prisoners began filing into town soon after the Battle of First Bull Run. The captured men were interred in Libby Prison, where they were effectively shut away from the rest of the population. Elizabeth had gotten in trouble with Richmond society soon after the war broke out, when she refused an invitation to join a group of ladies knitting flags and uniforms for the Confederate regiments. She took even more criticism when it became known that she was making regular visits to Libby Prison, where she aided the Union captives any way she could, bringing food, clothing, medicine and bedding. Proper Richmond women were outraged, yes, but what would they have thought if they knew what Elizabeth was *really* doing there?

While Elizabeth was all too happy aiding the wounded in Libby, humanitarian aid was just a cover. Elizabeth was actually there to collect any information prisoners had gleaned from behind enemy lines and pass it onto the Union brass in the field. Secretly questioning officers about Confederate numbers and movements that they had observed just before they were captured, Elizabeth would relay any information she got to Union intelligence. She did this with hidden messages that were carried by former Van Lew slaves who were loyal to the woman who had freed them. She tucked little notes into hollowed-out eggs that would be carried in a fellow conspirator's basket, or hid them in the false heels of boots. Her freed slaves were able to move back and forth across enemy lines with near impunity, and Elizabeth's information almost always reached its intended destination.

The war dragged on, and conditions grew evermore difficult in Richmond. Wealthy and poor alike found themselves facing food shortages, while practically everyday, casualty lists streamed into the city, leaving growing numbers of citizens brokenhearted at the sight of a loved one's name on the list of dead. Naturally, many of the citizens grew resentful of the Union men who were incarcerated in their city, and even more resentful of the woman who was showing so much concern for their well-being.

After a while, suspicions began to mount. People noticed that Elizabeth's visits to Libby had become almost a daily affair, and there was a bit too much traffic coming and going from the Van Lew household. Elizabeth had been able to keep the Libby guards in the dark with simple charm. She never showed up at the prison empty handed, dispensing gifts and kind words to the Confederate men who watched over the Northerners; very few bothered her about her administrations to their captives. Even the Prisoner Commandant held Elizabeth above suspicion.

Miss Van Lew took another tack with the prying eyes of Richmond's citizens. Becoming aware of her neighbors' whispered suspicions, she decided it was time to play up the "crazy" angle of her reputation. She was "Crazy Bet," after all. From then on, Elizabeth made a note to appear intentionally disheveled, putting on her most threadbare dresses when she went out and making sure her hair was always unkempt. On her daily walks to Libby Prison, Van Lew went further with her charade, muttering ceaseless gibberish to herself the entire way, consciously speaking louder and motioning at the air with exaggerated gesticulations when she walked by someone.

Her ruse worked. Suspicions about her visits to Libby faded, since no one was willing to believe that someone as unstable as Crazy Bet was capable of plotting any sort of espionage. Using her affected insanity as a cover, Elizabeth took on even greater operations. Even as she sent more and more messages out from captives to commanders, she also took to helping Union soldiers escape, going so far as to put captives up in her house until they could get safe transport out of Richmond. In 1864, Elizabeth grew so bold as to get her best friend and former slave, Mary Bowser, a job as a servant in the Confederate White House, home to none other than President Jefferson Davis. Here, Bowser was privy to all sorts of conversations between the Confederate president and senior military staff. Bowser passed everything she heard on to Van Lew, who in turn got the information out to Union brass. By the end of the war, Elizabeth's system of delivery got so efficient that Union General Ulysses Grant could depend on having flowers and intelligence reports from Richmond on his desk almost every day.

Of course, Elizabeth Van Lew picked the right side. When Grant's army marched into Richmond on April 1865, Elizabeth Van Lew wasted no time in raising the American flag over her home—she was through with playing crazy. None of her neighbors took this show of patriotism too well, and an angry mob quickly descended on her home. There was an ugly mood in the air, and many of the long-suffering Southerners were poised to do something drastic. Elizabeth emerged from her house and stood in front of the angry throng.

"Crazy Bet, you crazy old spinster!" someone yelled from the crowd. "You best take that Yankee rag down off your house, or we just might burn the whole place down!"

That was when Elizabeth stepped forward, standing clear-eyed and straight, nothing at all like the babbling lunatic they had all come to know. A hush fell over the crowd as she pointed a stern finger at the man who had shouted at her. "I know you, sir; I know where your family lives." Her eyes turned to another of the faces before her.

"I know you as well, and you," she pointed to yet another. "In fact I know most of you, who are so kind to pay me a visit. Let me assure you all that General Grant will be here in less than an hour, and if anyone does a single thing to my home or anyone housed in its walls, I promise you that person's own house will be burned to the ground before noon!"

While some might have doubted that Van Lew had those kinds of connections, no one was especially eager to test these doubts, and the crowd quickly dispersed after Elizabeth issued her threat. Sure enough, one of Grant's staff officers arrived at the Van Lew residence soon after that, asking if she was in need of provisions or protection. Van Lew looked at the Union soldier proudly. "I have gotten by all these years without any assistance. It would be strange to ask for a guard now that my friends are here, would it not?"

Bravery or naïveté? It is impossible to say what sort of life Elizabeth was expecting after the war. On the one hand, Grant publicly acknowledged the value of her efforts on behalf of the Union and had her appointed Postmistress of Richmond when he was elected president. Defeat sat heavily on Richmond in the Reconstruction years after the Civil War, and next to no one was willing to forgive Elizabeth Van Lew for aiding the enemy.

She never had too many friends to begin with; her vocal anti-slavery views alienated most of her contemporaries before the war. But when the people of Richmond learned about her undercover work, she became an out-and-out pariah. It was as if the entire city decided all at once that she didn't exist. No one visited and not a soul acknowledged her when she was in public. Former acquaintances wouldn't so much as nod if she called out to them on the street. For all intents and purposes, she became invisible, a living ghost that people loathed, shunned and eventually forgot.

By all accounts, Elizabeth was profoundly miserable for the rest of her days. She had fought for the abolition of slavery for so long, but the fruition of her lifelong ambition left her purposeless and hated. She lived through the rest of the 19th century, gradually falling into poverty after her stint as Postmistress expired.

During the last decade of her life, Elizabeth was practically unrecognizable from her former vivacious self. Years of idleness and isolation stripped her of much of her energy and intelligence. When she wasn't cooped up in her grand home on Grace Street, she could be seen walking aimlessly through her neighborhood. Long-since accustomed to being ignored, old Elizabeth didn't say a word to anyone while she went on her walks, hobbling by pedestrians without so much as a glance. Ironically, she acquired the habit of talking to herself in her later years, and her constant muttering brought back her old sobriquet, as new generations of Virginians took to calling her Crazy Bet.

Elizabeth Van Lew died in 1900, at the age of 82. She had fulfilled her life's goal nearly 35 years before her life ended and lived the rest of her years paying a heavy price for her convictions. She was buried in Richmond's Shockoe Cemetery, underneath a gravestone donated from admirers in Boston. It reads:

She risked everything that is dear to man—friends, fortune, comfort, health, life itself, all for one absorbing desire of her heart—that slavery might be abolished and the Union preserved.

But her story does not end there. The sightings began shortly after her death, when residents living on Grace Street spied the emaciated figure of old Crazy Bet hobbling down the same road she did when she was alive. She was seen only in the evening, instantly recognizable by every dumbfounded witness, manically making her way to some unknown destination. Many turned and ran from the shambling apparition, horrified at the sight of Crazy Bet coming back from the dead. Yet those who overcame their fear and endeavored to take a closer look were always disappointed. For after walking no more than three blocks, Crazy Bet would just vanish into the air.

Elizabeth's apparition continued to be reported until 1911, the year her home was demolished. After that, her supernatural jaunts all but ceased. And while there have been isolated sightings of a strange-looking woman wearing a hopelessly anachronistic dress since then, they have been so far and few between that it would be a stretch to say that the ghost of Van Lew or anyone else currently haunts Grace Street. Yet it could be that Crazy Bet's spirit occasionally returns to the city that despised her so, if not to visit her family home, perhaps to admire Richmond's lights sprawling underneath Grace Street while reflecting on her part in the eradication of slavery in the United States.

Phantom Crusader
HARPERS FERRY, WEST VIRGINIA

"I, John Brown, am now quite certain that the crimes of this guilty land will never be purged away but with blood."

These were John Brown's last words, not spoken, but written on a shred of paper that he passed to one of the guards flanking him as he was being led to the gallows. Standing ramrod straight and walking with almost enthusiastic resolution to his scaffold, Brown never once took his fierce gaze from the noose that had been tied, on that December 1859 morning, just for him. A guard of 1500 soldiers was standing at attention around the gallows outside Charles Town, Virginia, as a brisk winter wind blew over the desolate scene. Old John Brown went stoically, holding his bearded and bristling gray head high, seemingly indifferent to the fact that this dismal scene would mark the last moments of his life. Indeed, he seemed to be relishing it.

Bereft of a priest, Brown was led up to the gallows by the hangman, who took one uncertain look at the fierce old man before placing a hood over his head. The noose was tied around his neck, the signal given and the trapdoor sprung open. In the next instant, Brown was hanging from his broken neck, the once-fanatical abolitionist now nothing more than dead weight on the end of a taught rope. Or that is what many conservatives in the United States would have hoped, anyway. But almost everyone standing there knew, somewhere in their hearts, that John Brown's fanatical zeal against the slave-owning South, and the murderous manner in which he railed against the institution of slavery, was only a sign of the violence that was to come. John Brown knew he was being made into a martyr, that his execution would only deepen the divide between North and South. Sure enough, not two years after he was hanged, the Civil War had commenced, and the note that Brown passed to his guard made Brown into one of the United States' darkest prophets—and one of the nation's most celebrated killers.

Moved by a combination of religious zeal, hard-hearted egotism and mental instability, John Brown made his first strike against slavery on the evening of May 24, 1856. It was on that night that he and four followers went on their blood-soaked ride along the Pottawatomie Creek in eastern Kansas. They visited the homes of three prominent pro-slavery families, leaving mutilated bodies behind them at every stop. By the time they were finished, five men lay dead on the Kansas prairie, and John Brown was the face of a new, militant anti-slavery.

The following years saw Brown rubbing shoulders with leading members of the New England abolitionists as he lobbied for funds to bankroll further operations in the South. He spoke of leading a slave insurrection, of a nation-wide self-emancipation movement that would sweep across the Southern states like a Biblical scourge, eradicating the institution of slavery once and for all. That Brown's scourge meant mass murder deterred some of the more moderate abolitionists, but many New England socialites were willing to back his bloody enterprise. By

1859, he was ready for another strike—this one, however, was far more ambitious.

Harpers Ferry was a small village on the easternmost reaches of West Virginia, where the Potomac River meets the Shenandoah. Brown deemed it the ideal place to launch his uprising. He and his group of 21 men would raid the United States arsenal in town, confiscate the arms there and then sit back and wait as legions of angry slaves flocked to their banner of emancipation. Brown wasn't too clear on the details. He did not bother with a detailed strategy, made no provision for error and didn't even get word out to Virginia slaves that the attack on Harpers Ferry was even taking place. As far as Brown was concerned, as long as his intentions were pure, God would take care of the rest. His faith was unshakable.

But as it turned out, even if God really did have an opinion on slavery in the South, He wasn't too interested in Brown's attack on Harpers Ferry. The raid that Brown assumed would lead to the ultimate dissolution of slavery was over less than 36 hours after it had begun. While Brown's gang did manage to take the arsenal, the towns-folk grew wise to the operation soon after Brown's men occupied the building, and instead of drawing thousands of rebellious slaves to his banner, Brown only attracted scores of armed and angry Southerners. Citizens promptly formed a militia and surrounded the arsenal; it was not long before a roaring gunfight between the surrounding Virginians and Brown's besieged raiders was in full effect. The battle lasted all through the day, until a company of United States Marines arrived from Washington on the morning of October 18, 1859. Under

John Brown, a violent abolitionist, was hanged after a failed munitions raid in Harpers Ferry, West Virginia.

the command of then Lieutenant Colonel Robert E. Lee—the same Robert E. Lee who later led the Confederate Army during the Civil War—the Marines stormed the building and engaged the raiders in close combat. Once the Marines were inside, the fighting lasted only a few minutes.

And so it was that John Brown, the self-proclaimed soldier of God, ended up at the mercy of a Virginian judge. Not that he recognized the judge's authority or supplicated for his mercy at any time during the trial. In fact, Brown's staunch commitment to his cause remained so solid during his incarceration that even as many Americans were dismissing Brown as a homicidal zealot, others were admiring him for the strength of his convictions. In the end, Brown understood well the effect his martyrdom would have, and forecast, correctly, the coming Civil War. No one would forget his sacrifice. "John Brown's Body" became a popular Union marching song throughout the war, and the eye of American history acknowledged the raid on Harpers Ferry as yet another polarizing factor that led to the ultimate division of the nation into the Union and Confederate camps.

The memory of John Brown's attack on Harpers Ferry lost much of its fire after the Civil War ended. With Northern victory came Americans' desire to put behind them the sectionalism and violence that had so recently wreaked havoc. The war was over, slavery was banished, the country wanted to forget and John Brown's martyrdom lost its popular virulence. The once-celebrated crusader was relegated to a historical footnote, and people all across the country tried to get on with their lives. Yet many citizens living in Harpers Ferry quickly came to realize that sometimes history wasn't so easy to let go— that sometimes, the past itself seemed to *want* to hold on, whether people wanted it or not. Such was the case with the ghost of John Brown.

No one knows who saw him first, nor on what exact day, but it is said that he appeared in Harpers Ferry not long after the Civil War was over, walking innocuously, if somewhat ominously, down the streets of the small West Virginia village. He did not appear "ghostly." That is, he looked to be completely solid, his features as sharp as a living man's; no part of him was transparent or cloaked in mist, as is so often the case with phantoms. Consistently appearing at dusk, just as the southern sky began to darken, the fierce old abolitionist walked casually, with a levity in his step that he never possessed when he was alive. Superficially, he looked to be the same murdering curmudgeon that he always was, with his grizzled hair, bristling beard and strong, sinewy build. Yet witnesses who looked closer, into his eyes, saw a strange kind of joy there—as if the man walking before them was filled with a deep sense of self-satisfaction. This was no angry abolitionist bent on incalculable vengeance, but a pleased old man taking in the quaint southern town around him. At his side walked a small black dog that always kept perfect time with the long stride of its master.

One might only imagine the shock that accompanied early sightings of John Brown. A dreadful icon from an unwelcome past, Brown represented death and difficulty to the few people who remained in Harpers Ferry after the war, and his appearance was considered a bad omen. Some turned and ran when they saw the vigorous old phantom approaching. Others were said to follow him cautiously, perhaps intending to give the old man a piece of their mind, or maybe hoping to plead with him to leave their town in peace. But Brown always managed to elude

Brown's ghost still wanders the streets of Harpers Ferry, often accompanied by his small black dog.

confrontation before a word was said—vanishing around a street corner, into some bushes or down an alley just as he was being approached. Disappearing as quickly as he appeared, Brown's apparition never did anyone any harm. Nevertheless, he was hardly a welcome presence in the streets of Harpers Ferry. Not at first, anyway.

Yet time went on, and as one generation succeeded another, the ghost of old John Brown earned a certain acceptance among the locals. His appearances grew less and less common, but whenever he was spotted the joyful glow in his brilliant blue eyes seemed to be evermore pronounced. True, there were very few people living in the small town, which never recovered from the devastation of the Civil War. Every year, there were fewer and fewer people living in Harpers Ferry, but those who tried to make lives for themselves in the West Virginia burg perceived the dead abolitionist as the dilapidated town's mascot. "There goes Old Man Brown," some local would say at the sight of the anachronistic apparition as he made his way down a street with his small black dog trotting at his side. "At least he hasn't up and left town yet."

In the 1950s, the National Park Service realized the historical importance of the decaying town and undertook the work of restoration. Their efforts were well rewarded. Today, Harpers Ferry is one of the country's most popular National Historic Sites, drawing in close to two million visitors a year, many of whom leave with a new understanding of the Civil War and the factors that led up to it.

A smaller number end up experiencing more history than they might have expected. Sightings of a mysterious old man walking through town at dusk with a black dog at his side are reported about once or twice a year. Many who see the gray-haired man in his 19th-century attire assume that he is a John Brown impersonator working for the park, and they stop him for a photograph. Remarkably, the man is known to stop, and in complete silence acquiesce to having his picture taken. The man moves on without a word as soon as the shutter snaps shut, rounding the first corner that he reaches. Over the years, hundreds of tourists have encountered the John Brown "impersonator" and his black dog, but not one of them has any photographic proof, because in every picture taken of him there is only a strange illuminated blur where he should be standing. It is now generally accepted that this is the ghost of John Brown.

And according to those who have seen him, the legendary abolitionist's ghost seems to be quite happy. If this is puzzling to history buffs who have read about Brown's austere devotion and dour disposition while alive, could it be that Brown has been able to temper the harder aspects of his character in the afterlife? This is entirely possible, since Brown's lifelong goal, the abolition of slavery, came to pass a few years after he was executed. Perhaps, then, his spirit remains in Harpers Ferry, perpetually celebrating the sacrifice that he and members of his group of 21 made so many years ago, a sacrifice that, John Brown's ghost might believe, was not made in vain.

The Phantom Rider
CLAY COUNTY, WEST VIRGINIA

A good number of histories have looked back on the Civil War with fawning eyes. Florid narratives have embossed the bloody engagements in martial pageantry, where the combatants, driven by high ideals and unflinching bravery, stood above the roaring madness of battle by virtue of individual acts of heroism. So goes the jingoistic paean of war, making heroes from horrific bloodletting. It is certainly true that the dire circumstances of the Civil War did bring out the best in many men—men whose actions were able to turn the godforsaken tableau before them into an exhibition of humanity's most esteemed virtues. Yet there is also the flip side of the story, where the horrors of war were just that—plain and simple horrors.

Away from the martial glorification of violence there was another kind of reality to the Civil War, where the dissolution of civilian order allowed men's baser qualities to thrive. In many regions, disorder and deprivation ruled the day, might became the only right and murder was the only currency that really mattered. This was the uglier face of the conflict, often hid from the wide-open battlefields of national myth. This version of the Civil War preferred the backcountry—the areas where the divide between North and South was far less certain and armed men were able to go unchecked by any formal military authority—in the hills, woods and hidden groves of the American wild where bushwhackers and guerillas did their dirty work.

This was how much of the fighting in West Virginia played out. A hotbed of political antagonism, the state of West Virginia was born out of local representatives' refusal to go along with the Virginia Assembly's bill for secession in April 1861. It was then that a cluster of counties in the Allegheny Highland of Western Virginia came together, wrote their own constitution and formed the pro-Union state that still exists today. While Abraham Lincoln eagerly accepted this recalcitrant Southern offshoot into the Union fold, the movement was far from universally accepted amongst the people of the new state. If there were a number of West Virginians who believed secession amounted to treason, so too were there a number unhappy about breaking off from the Old Dominion and willing to fight for the Confederacy.

Aware of the divisiveness in the new Mountain State, and none too happy about its official siding with the Union, Virginia Governor John Letcher put together guerrilla bands ordered to disrupt Union activity in West Virginia any way they could. He also commissioned a number of agents to make their way behind enemy lines and form gangs of bushwhackers in areas where Confederate sympathies ran high. So it was that the fighting men of West Virginia were mobilized into two opposing camps, and the fighting spread out all over the hilly countryside, engulfing every man, woman and child in its path.

It was not long into the violence when many of the gangs of fighters lost their moorings and took to attacking whomever they wanted, as long as there was personal gain to be had from it. Confederate sympathizers in West Virginia were soon complaining that Governor Letcher's bushwhackers raided them as often as they did Union supporters and neutrals. And so it was that so many of the Confederate irregulars became regarded as little more than highwaymen taking advantage of the lawless conditions in the Appalachians. The Union guerrillas were often no better, marauding the hills of West Virginia, leaving a wide swath of death and destruction behind them.

If the fighting in West Virginia was motivated as much by opportunity as by political allegiance, there was still enough ire for the enemy that any man running into a gang from the other side was as good as dead. Any West Virginian soldier returning home on furlough was taking his life in his hands. It was hard for a Union or Confederate regular to know if the house he was returning to was in friendly territory or if it belonged to the enemy. The hillsides were littered with the bodies of West Virginia soldiers who were bushwhacked by their enemies on their way home.

According to local legend, one such unfortunate was a young man whose name history has forgotten. He was a tired Confederate soldier on leave, returning to his parents' home in Clay County, looking forward to a short reprieve from the madness of the eastern battlefields. While he would have known about the dangerous situation in West Virginia, warnings of danger lurking in the hills were lost on this man, who had spent the previous year staring down Union riflemen and artillery barrages. He had grown familiar with death; he had stood by and watched as it took scores of men around him. He had rubbed shoulders with it on more than one battlefield, and while his experiences did nothing to lessen his fear of it, he was more than willing to take the risk, if only to see his home again.

His return home was joyous, marred only by his mother's excessive concern. She wept in joy when she saw her boy again, but wept also in fear, for Clay County was controlled by an especially vicious group of Union guerrillas, and was no longer safe for anyone who stood by the Stars and Bars. The soldier's mother implored him to leave right away, but the boy would not. "I didn't come all the way out here just to turn around and run back on account of a few Yanks hiding in the hills," the young man said. "Ain't no way I'm leavin' now, at least not until I see my girl again."

His girl was another reason the Confederate had returned home. Engaged to be married when the war broke out, the soldier threw in his lot with old Virginia and found himself going off to war before he was able to marry his one and only. Now, after two years of fighting, he was back, and no man or affiliation of men—armed or otherwise—was going to keep him from his fiancée.

He went to visit her on the second night he was back, creeping through the darkness until he was crouched against her bedroom wall, gingerly tapping on the windowpane until she woke up. Well, if there was any danger, the visit that night made the trip worthwhile. The long-separated couple stayed up to the early hours; he unloaded all the inhumanity he witnessed since he had seen her last, while she explained how hard things had been at home for the last two years. They talked for the entire night, the young man barely able to tear himself away when the morning sun began to creep into the sky.

By the time he finally did leave, something had changed in the Confederate's heart. The long-missed company of his betrothed had eased the weight he had been carrying for so long. Looking around him, he found himself noticing, for the first time in a long time, the spectacular pallet of the morning's sky, the lush green of the dew-soaked leaves. Only then did he realize how dark his soul had been, how utterly hopeless he had become. That was the man who had sneaked into his fiancée's house the previous night; the man softly whistling on his

way back to his family's house was someone else alto-
gether.

Staying indoors for most of the day, the young man
was resolved to spend one more night with his betrothed
before rejoining his unit. Again, his mother bemoaned his
recklessness. She tried to convince her son of the danger
of his nocturnal foray. "My boy, there are Yankees in the
hills. It ain't safe. They've been killing our boys for as long
as this war's been on. I'm beggin' ya please. Don't go."

But the soldier again disregarded his mother's pleas.
Indeed, so emboldened was he by the ease of his visit the
night before, the Confederate decided to take his father's
horse this time around. "Don't worry about a thing, ma,"
he said as he flicked the reins of the old nag he sat upon.
"Ain't no way any dirty Yank's gonna catch me on this
charger." The soldier let out a giddy laugh and spurred his
father's old horse onto the road, turning around and waving to his mother and father just before he turned a corner and was out of sight. That was the last time they saw
their son alive.

There is no account of exactly what happened when he
reached the crossroads about two miles from his parents'
home. Did he see them coming? Was he surprised? Did he
try to run? Did he put up much of a fight? All that is
known for certain was that the young man was bushwhacked by a group of Union soldiers waiting in the
bushes at the crossroads. They slit his throat, tied him to
his father's horse and let the beast make its way back to its
master. It isn't necessary to narrate the reaction of the soldier's poor parents when they woke up the next morning

to find in their front yard the body of their son, tied to their blood-soaked horse.

His grief-stricken parents buried him beside the crossroads where he was murdered, and the soldier returning home on furlough became just another heartache in an era that was largely defined as such. Neither his fiancée nor his parents were ever the same again, and his story was canonized as one among many local tragedies that were inflicted upon the region from 1861 to 1865.

But time passed, and all who knew the young soldier eventually passed on, and the sad incident was preserved by word of mouth, transferred from generation to generation until it was embedded in the local folklore. Many heard the story about the dead Confederate from their elders, and many others had far more immediate experiences with the murdered soldier. For years after the Civil War was over, a good number of Clay County residents claimed to see the same Confederate soldier making his way along the same rough back road he was murdered on.

Spotted only at night, sometime between 9:30 and midnight, the young man was always said to be trotting down the road at a brisk pace, with a look of barely contained exuberance on his face. Nocturnal travelers who caught sight of him would always stop and stare in complete wonder, because even though the rider appeared as clear and as real as anyone else, his horse's hooves made no sound on the dirt road. The man's jaunty approach was completely silent.

He would continue to make his way down the road with the peculiar expression of joy on his face until he reached the same crossroads where the murder occurred.

It was then that the man's expression would change from bliss to alarm. At that moment, he would stand in his stirrups, cast one panicked look over his shoulder and then vanish from sight, without a trace or a warning, as if he was never there in the first place.

This sequence occurred more than once. In fact, it continued to be reported throughout the remainder of the 19th century and well into the 20th. The apparition always appeared in the evening on the same road and vanished in the same manner. The community was quick to draw the connection between the murdered soldier and the vanishing apparition. His death—cut down as he was on the way to his fiancée's house as he celebrated a rediscovered life—was certainly tragic enough to merit a haunting.

Yet for whatever reason, his apparition stopped appearing in Clark County shortly after the Second World War. No one can say for sure why the soldier's ageless apparition simply ceased to be. Maybe his spirit sensed that the monumental sacrifice of American men during that war superseded the loss he suffered so many years before, and he finally abandoned his tortured vigil over the road he died on. Or perhaps the time had simply come for him to get over the trauma of the event. Whatever the case, we may only hope that the young Confederate soldier has finally found his peace.

Dead Man on Dug Hill Road
SOUTHWEST ILLINOIS

The two Union soldiers lay flat in the bush, their hearts pounding heavily as they looked down the dirt road in front of them. A full moon shone in the clear summer sky, and the silvery darkness ominously blanketed every hamlet, farmhouse and field in the southwest tip of Illinois along with the two frightened men lying in the dark. They barely dared to breathe, so intent were they on listening to the sound of the approaching wagon, still invisible in the darkness.

The soldiers were actually ex-soldiers, two deserters who had had enough of the madness of the Civil War and decided to get out, hoping to start a new life in the wide-open territories of the Great Plains. The bloody contest had not yet been decided, but they had seen enough to decide that victory for either North or South wasn't worth the carnage of the war. Nothing was. They had been walking along Dug Hill Road, an old rural byway that wound across the southwest tip of Illinois, traveling only at night, careful to avoid the cities and towns along their way—all too conscious of the fact that their desertion from the Union was a crime punishable by death.

Neither man was too enthused about having his neck stretched at the end of a noose, and though they were weary of killing, they would not hesitate to turn their guns against anyone who tried to turn them in. They were risking their lives, creeping across Illinois to get away from the carnage of the East, with its blood-soaked battlefields. But they were willing to do whatever it took, even kill, to get out alive.

They had stayed out of sight thus far, limiting their traveling to the evening hours and hiding in the bush by the side of the road whenever they heard someone approaching. They had almost made it across Illinois without being seen and had come to equate the silent darkness of the state's rural back country with safety. On this night, the sounds of chirping crickets and boots on the gravel road were broken by the sound of something approaching from behind. Horses' hooves fell on the dirt surface of Dug Hill Road and a wooden wagon creaked and strained as it bumped over the path.

The two deserters moved in near-simultaneous motion, disappearing noiselessly into the bushes on the side of the road. There they lay and waited, staring down the road with bated breath. The moon shone, cold and unforgiving, on the scene below—the two men in the bush, the meandering dirt road and the suddenly visible wagon, pulled by two horses, with a single man perched over the reins. He was right in front of them: a lone Union military officer in a wagon steering his two horses down the road. They could make out the man's rank in the moonlight; he was a provost marshal, a senior officer of the military police. If they should ever be apprehended, a man of his rank would preside over their court martial. Their potential executioner was riding unknowingly right in front of them, completely at their mercy. Caught up in the irony of the situation, the two deserters looked at each other in the darkness and shared twisted smiles.

Two Union deserters killed an officer during the war, causing his ghost to haunt Dug Hill Road in southern Illinois.

And then they noticed the officer's horses. The two Union mounts looked better fed than the two men were, and again, their minds came together with the same thought. *Transportation*. The pair were starting to get quite close to the Missouri line, but there were still a lot of miles to cover if the men hoped to make it into Kansas. Two horses would definitely help them make it there quicker. They looked from where the wagon passed and into each other's eyes. Both knew what the other was thinking. A few tense seconds dripped by before one of the men made the decision for the other, jerking his head at the officer on the road and slowly running his index finger across his throat. The other man nodded. It was survival after all.

In the next instant, the two men charged out of the bush. They boarded the provost marshal's wagon before the officer knew what was going on. He registered the gleam of one assailant's knife in the moonlight and went for his revolver, but by the time his palm clasped the handle, a pair of strong, desperate arms were locked around his shoulders. One of the deserters pulled the marshal down while the other ran the edge of his knife over his throat. The work was over in a few merciless moments, completed with brutal efficiency; both deserters had killed before.

Pushing the marshal off the wagon while the blood still gurgled from the deep gash in his throat, the two men whipped the horses into a gallop and were gone. The Union officer lay on his back in a quickly spreading pool of his own blood. He made a futile attempt to cover the gaping wound, but to no avail; the blood gurgled forth between his fingers and into the dirt.

His body was found by a local who was driving down the road the very next day, and the officer was promptly given a state burial. As for the two deserters, there is no record of how they fared in the West or even if they got there at all.

While the pair vanished from the historical record, the provost marshal who met his end on Dug Hill Road has lingered on well past his time, constantly reminding Union County residents in southern Illinois of the crime that occurred there during the Civil War. Or perhaps it might be more accurate to say that some part of the officer has remained behind on the spot where he was killed, much to the dismay of those commuters who have had the misfortune of running into him.

He was first spotted by an elderly farmer a few days after he was buried, lying in the same position that he was originally found in—sprawled in the middle of the road in a dark pool of his own blood, staring blankly at the sky above him. The old man assumed that he was looking at another casualty of the conflict. Getting off his wagon to see if there was anything he could do, the farmer had not walked far when the corpse slowly began to vanish, becoming transparent right in front of him. He hadn't made it another five paces before the figure had faded into nothingness.

It was the first of many sightings of the dead man on Dug Hill Road. Over the years, this same apparition was reported countless times. Residents of Jonesboro, about 5 miles east of the scene of the murder, have long accepted the presence of the ghost on the nearby thoroughfare. He was there when horses took people wherever they needed to go along Illinois' roads, and continues to be spotted today in the age of automobiles. Indeed it seems that the ghost of the dead marshal is seen more than ever now, even though Dug Hill Road is a paved section of Highway 146, and the Civil War has long run its course.

Not only is the body of the dead officer seen on the road, but on many occasions, late-night commuters have spotted a phantom wagon being pulled by two horses along the shoulder of the highway, slowly making its way west towards the Mississippi River. It is obvious to awestruck motorists that this is not a typical buggy, for not only does it glow with an ethereal silver light, but there is no driver steering it. The horses move on their own, proceeding slowly in their 19th-century harnesses. Those drivers who have stopped alongside the spectral wagon to get a closer look claim that they can hear the sound of the horses' hooves on the road. The plodding pace continues as the wagon slowly begins to fade into nothingness. After about 20 yards, the wagon is clearly transparent and the sound of the hooves is extremely faint, as if coming from a great distance. A moment later, the wagon and horses vanish, leaving motorists on Highway 146 staring into the empty night.

4
Public
Hauntings

Ghosts of the Michigan Dead
GRAND RAPIDS, MICHIGAN

Out of respect for the American veterans that currently reside there, Nicole Bray, founder of the West Michigan Ghost Hunters Society, prefers not to disclose the exact location of this haunted cemetery. Suffice to say that it is located in a midsize town in western Michigan and has been considered haunted for many years. "People have been talking about the Michigan Soldiers' Home for quite some time," Nicole says, "we've received a lot of emails from people who've had run-ins with ghosts there, and the cemetery is often brought up during seminars on local hauntings."

There were no battles fought in Michigan, but it is estimated that over 90,000 men from the Great Lakes State enlisted to fight for the Union, of which nearly 15,000 perished. These men are buried in cemeteries all across Michigan, their all-but-forgotten sacrifices enshrined under all-but-forgotten monuments. They are almost forgotten, but not entirely.

The Michigan Soldiers' Home was formed soon after the Civil War to provide a home for wounded veterans who were unable to support themselves after the conflict. A residence to over 300 veterans during its first year of operation, the Home continued to grow throughout the 19th century, eventually housing twice the number of its original occupants. Along with the Soldiers' Home, the Michigan authority set aside 5 acres for soldiers who had passed on. The cemetery grounds were arranged as a

Maltese Cross, with over 200 burial sites clustered into each of the cross' four ends. In 1894, the state commissioned a statue of a Civil War soldier to be erected in the center, a final monument to the war that shaped the United States and to those men who gave their lives to it. Today, the bodies of close to 4000 soldiers from other wars lie buried there next to their Civil War brethren. Yet though the Civil War dead are outnumbered nearly 20 to 1, they are the ones that get most of the attention from Michiganders. For of all the dead interred there, they are the only ones that are said to get up and walk around.

The bizarre incidents at the Michigan Soldiers' Home have been going on for as long as anyone can remember and continue to be reported on a regular basis today. "We're always hearing stories about the Michigan Soldiers' Home," Nicole says. "Workers there have written us about unexplained cold spots, intense feelings of being watched, weird noises, footsteps and strange electrical disturbances."

These phenomena have occurred only in the proximity of the Civil War gravesites. Through the years, employees wishing to stay on at the Michigan Soldiers' Home have had to acquire thick skin around the Civil War burial sites and learn to ignore the unnatural goings-on that regularly occur. Yet while many have been able to disregard disembodied footsteps, inexplicable moans, sudden chills and mysteriously failing flashlights, others have witnessed events that they would never be able to forget.

These are the men and women who have run into the cemetery's supernatural sentries walking amid the gravestones of their brothers in arms. Appearing as semi-transparent apparitions shrouded in mist, the ghosts of the Michigan Soldiers' Home make their rounds only at night, drifting over the burial ground in ominous silence. These guards are obscured by the darkness and the tendrils of mist that wind around them. But enough of their features are visible for witnesses to make out that they are Union soldiers from the Civil War era—their blue caps and brass buttons faintly perceptible in the darkness, the tips of their bayoneted rifles, carried at the shoulder, glimmering dull and gray in the night. Sometimes these apparitions are visible for only a few minutes, on other occasions they remain for the better part of the evening, keeping up their ghostly vigil over the burial plots of their fellow soldiers.

This is one theory. Nicole Bray's West Michigan Ghost Hunters are well aware of the haunting at the Michigan Soldiers' Home, but the group's full schedule of supernatural investigations has not allowed time for a thorough inquiry into the phenomena occurring there. "We've heard so much about the Michigan Soldiers Home," Nicole says, "but we haven't been able to make our way over there yet." Perhaps these paranormal enthusiasts will shed some light on the situation when they are able to make their way to the Soldiers' Home.

Until then, visitors to the old military cemetery who have had run-ins with the supernatural sentries there will have to satisfy themselves with supposition. Did these phantom soldiers have specific experiences while they were alive that prompted them to continue their vigil after death? Or perhaps these spirits are some sort of manifestation of all the Civil War dead buried at the Soldiers'

Home. Could it be that the ghosts that eyewitnesses have glimpsed are not apparitions of any specific soldier, but rather, stand as supernatural symbols of the collective loss suffered by these early Michigan dead? No one can say for certain.

The mystery surrounding the ghosts of the Soldiers' Home only piques Nicole Bray's interest. "We are really looking forward to getting over there," Nicole says. "It's probably one of the most talked about local hauntings, but there's very little information about it." No doubt that will change after the West Michigan Ghost Hunters get a chance to investigate the site.

Martha Washington Inn
ABINGDON, VIRGINIA

Abingdon, Virginia, has a lasting love affair with the Washingtons, both George and Martha. It's the county seat for Washington County, established by the General Assembly of Virginia in 1776 as the first region named for the famed general and president. Abingdon itself drew its name from Abingdon Parrish, Martha Washington's English home, and one of the town's most beloved and treasured institutions is the Martha Washington Inn. Here, in this 171-year-old building that has borne Martha Washington's name for so many years, another love affair continues to play itself out, even though its players departed this earth so many years ago. The Martha

Washington Inn may be famous for its four-star rating, dedicated staff, period furniture and fine Virginia cuisine, but for many, the Martha Washington Inn is better known as the home of Beth Smith. Beth Smith died in 1862, but she lives on in story and memory. She is a ghost, after all, whose appearances in history-loving Abingdon are treasured.

In the early 19th century, Abingdon had evolved into a well-established community and an economic center for southwest Virginia. Brigadier General Francis Preston was familiar with Abingdon, having visited years before, and as he thought about where he should spend his retirement, he could think of no other place than the seat of Washington County. And so it was that in 1832 Preston moved to Abingdon and built himself a home on what would become West Main Street. The place was immense, a mansion really, more space than any one man needed. When Preston died, the home was purchased for the schooling of young women. The first classes in the Martha Washington College for Women (the first such recognition of Washington's wife) began in March of 1860.

Classes were interrupted, however, by the start of the Civil War and as many of that war's battles were fought in the state of Virginia, few Virginia towns escaped the war unscathed. Abingdon was not one of them. As the walking wounded limped into town and others were carried in on stretchers, the people of Abingdon realized that they had a duty to serve their country, the Confederate States of America. The wounded and sick were given beds and rooms in the Martha Washington College, and nurses and doctors replaced the young women who had, just weeks before, been studying in the classrooms.

One of the nurses brought in to tend to the ill was Beth Smith, a girl who was recruited to work as a nurse even though she was too young to deal with the horrors of war. Her innocence was a necessary sacrifice of the war and it was shed the moment she found John Stoves wounded and bloody. The 20-year-old Confederate captain had been shot numerous times and he lay in the street, calling out feebly for help. Beth heard him and ran to the makeshift hospital where she summoned the doctors. Unfortunately, with Union activity running high in Abingdon, they had to wait until they could move under the cover of darkness before tending to the Confederate fighter.

Stoves lost so much blood that by the time doctors were able to reach him, he was shaking uncontrollably. They carried him to the makeshift hospital, taking a cir-cuitous route in the hopes of evading capture. Mercifully, Stoves had succumbed to his pain, unconsciousness bless-ing him with relief.

He awoke to find himself in a large room. Some say it was what is now Room 403 and others claim it's Room 302. Regardless, he found himself under the care of the nurse who had rescued him. Beth had dedicated herself to Stoves' recovery. She couldn't explain why or how, but something about his eyes touched something deep within her. Their mournful and tragic beauty captivated her. And so it was that she had spent an evening tending to the cap-tain's wounds and to his comfort. She kept his hand in hers, so that he might know he was not alone when he awoke. When he did, he might have believed the young woman mopping his brow was an angel and he wouldn't have been terribly mistaken.

Every spare moment the girl had, she was by Stoves' side. When there was nothing else she could do to comfort him, she brought out her violin. She was a skilled musician, and her playing lifted the spirits of all those around her, except those of the man for whom she played. Most could see that the girl had fallen in love with the dashing Confederate captain, but they knew that it had to end in tragedy.

The soldier was not recovering. As death approached, Stoves motioned for Beth to continue playing her violin. Play she did, stopping only to call nurses and doctors to his side when he began shaking uncontrollably. As doctors worked to save the captain's life, she continued to play, and it was to her music that Stoves passed away. She continued to play long after doctors had covered his body with a sheet; she refused to believe that he had died. She was convinced that he would wake up, that the doctors were mistaken. When people came to take Stoves' body away to make room for others wounded in battle, Beth fought them, throwing herself on top of him.

Then, according to writer Kristin Rothwell, a breeze blew through the room, extinguishing all the candles. Plunged into darkness, Beth and the doctors couldn't help noticing the bright light that appeared across the room and that began to float across the room towards them. As the light approached, Beth saw that it was a figure, a woman dressed in the whitest of white robes, who did just one thing before vanishing. She told Beth that she had done her best and that she had cared for Stoves but that he had indeed died. Stoves was laid to rest in a cemetery.

Beth continued to work in the makeshift hospital, and her dedication may have led to her death. She contracted typhoid fever, and the doctors did what they could to make their dedicated young nurse comfortable. Her room was familiar; after all, it was Stoves' old room. Beth died in the same room, just weeks after the captain's death. Not surprisingly, considering all the trauma and tragedy in her life, Beth did not go into death quietly.

Ever since her passing, the room where she died has become the home of what many believe to be Beth's spirit. When students returned to Martha Washington College, many reported hearing violin music playing in the hallways. The spirit is determined, the people of Abingdon believe, to remind the living of her love and devotion to her dying soldier. To that end, her violin playing can still be heard throughout the hallways of the Martha Washington Inn. Those staying in her old room have not only heard her violin's plaintive call, but also have seen her apparition enter the room and sit down next to the bed. One hopes that Beth's death has reunited her with her dead soldier love, but if not, then one suspects that she is not starved for attention living in the Martha Washington Inn.

In addition to the numbers of tourists who come to stay in any of the inn's rooms or suites, there are the other permanent guests of the inn. One is a Confederate soldier who was shot and killed in the building as he ran up the steps to warn the other Confederates of the rapidly approaching Union army. He had just reached the upper landing when shots rang out, and he collapsed to the floor. His blood stained the floorboards, leading to a most interesting phenomenon that a veteran bellhop at the inn has noticed. Over 30 years, he has noticed that whenever carpets are changed on the landing, they acquire holes where the man's blood was spilled. Random cold spots in the building are all too common, as are doors that open on their own and wispy figures that appear and disappear out of the air.

Outside, visitors and staff have reported seeing a horse with no rider pace back and forth in front of the inn's entrance, waiting, it seems, for its rider to return. By all accounts, the horse has been waiting for a century and a half and will probably continue to wait for many more years. The horse began his vigil during the Civil War, when his rider, a Union soldier, was shot to death in front of the college. It's believed that the horse appears only on moonless nights. Even among all these spirits, it is still Beth's that attracts the most attention. Her story is the Martha Washington Inn's most poignant and tragic, and years after Captain Stoves' and Beth Smith's deaths, the account still resonates. Visitors still come to Abingdon and its storied Martha Washington Inn, hoping to hear a snatch of Beth's haunting melodies or to catch a glimpse of the brokenhearted girl herself.

Andersonville
ANDERSONVILLE, GEORGIA

When planners first arrived in Andersonville in 1864, they were convinced that they had found the ideal site for a new Confederate prison. The new facility was sorely needed; prisons in Richmond, Virginia, were already over-crowded, and if the prison population were to escape, it could easily overwhelm the Confederate capital. Word arrived that Union General Ulysses S. Grant would no longer be exchanging prisoners; each soldier he held was one less who could reinforce the Confederate ranks. The number of Union soldiers in captivity continued to rise.

Confederate Captains W. Sidney Winder and Boyce Charwick arrived in Georgia in November 1863. They walked in and around Sumter County, near the town of Andersonville. Here, they found a site that was far removed from the Union army. The area was served by the Georgia Southwestern Railway and sat amidst thick stands of pine trees that would be useful for the construction of the stockade, barracks and hospital. The lumber would supply prisoners with the fuel necessary to make fires and cook their food. Running through the proposed site was the Sweetwater Creek, which would serve as both well and bath for the prisoners.

The Confederate government planned to build a prison to house 10,000 captured Union soldiers. The site appeared perfect. Unfortunately, rarely is the ideal met and over the next 14 months, over 40,000 Union prisoners were to stay at Andersonville. Over 12,000 would never walk beyond its walls. Life was worse than death in Andersonville and many begged for the Reaper's touch just to have sweet release from the filthy, overcrowded conditions where dead bodies lay stacked in piles next to the living.

Not surprisingly, with such a history steeped in the macabre and the grotesque, Andersonville is a haunted place. People say the very ground the prison sat on is forever tainted with the scent of death. Nothing save for the odd patch of grass and brush grows upon the land. Only the dead walk here, the most controversial of whom is Henry Wirz. Reviled as a heartless wretch by some, seen as a scapegoat by others, Wirz is the only American ever executed for war crimes against other Americans.

How did Andersonville happen? Some say it was mismanagement; others say it was a deliberate and calculated bit of cruelty. Certainly it wasn't the only Civil War prison to experience death and brutality within its walls (after all, Elmira, a federal prison in New York, had a death rate that came close to matching Andersonville's), but it was the one that was brought to the public's attention and that galvanized public opinion. When the survivors of Andersonville were liberated in 1865, photographs of these men, who were little more than walking skeletons, appeared in *Harper's Weekly*. The hell they brought into the homes of millions demanded a reaction and they got one. People were angry and incensed. They demanded retribution and they got it.

The government brought charges against Confederate General Robert E. Lee, Secretary of War James Seddon and others of deliberately trying to kill the captured

The cemetery at Andersonville; thousands succumbed to disease and malnutrition during incarceration.

soldiers. It didn't help that Wirz's commander, Brigadier General John H. Winder, believed that all Union soldiers should die and that he was proud of the fact that more of them were dying in Andersonville than on the battlefield. But President Andrew Johnson ordered all charges be dropped against all Confederate generals and politicians, leaving Captain Henry Wirz, Andersonville's commandant, alone to slake the thirst of a nation eager for justice. Wirz was a condemned man.

He appeared before a military commission on August 21, 1865. His trial revealed an Andersonville almost no one had the stomach to hear about. The commissioners learned how 32,000 Union soldiers were crammed into a space built for only 10,000. Even an expansion to 26 acres failed to arrest the overcrowding. They heard about the ironically named Sweetwater Creek that ran through the site. Meant to provide soldiers with drinking and bathing water, it had become stagnant and poisonous because its flow was not strong enough to carry away into the river the tremendous volume of human waste deposited by 32,000 men. To compound matters, Confederate planners had built the guard and hospital buildings upstream and these facilities threw all their garbage, be it human or animal waste, into the river too. Soldiers had no choice but to drink from this noxious stew and developed dysentery and diarrhea as a result.

The commission was told how prisoners walked and slept beneath the elements, how they baked during the day beneath the hot Georgian sun and spent the night exposed. After all, they were forbidden to construct shelters. Blankets were all they had. Medical treatment was nonexistent; scurvy and dysentery were taking men by the thousands. Those whom disease didn't take, starvation claimed. And those who lived could barely move with their limbs pulled tightly around their bodies from scurvy. Others had had limbs amputated, gangrenous as they were from coming in contact with the water of Sweetwater Creek.

As it was, there was barely enough food in the South to feed the Confederate army, and it was the prisoners who suffered. They were given a daily ration of a meager amount of corn meal, some meat and, if they were fortunate, some beans, peas or rice. Alas, so many no longer had teeth that eating solid food was almost impossible. They could only eat concoctions like beef tea with boiled rice. Corn bread caused diseased gums to bleed and teeth to fall out.

Under these impoverished conditions, over 100 prisoners a day were dying, whether from disease or starvation or exposure. There were even those who were killed by other prisoners, desperate perhaps for more food or clothing. With so many dead, many were left where they died to lie among the living. The scent of decaying flesh hung over Andersonville like a funeral shroud. It was constant and as inescapable as the moans, groans and cries of the ailing that rent the air both day and night.

Prisoners attempting to escape this hell on earth were to be shot the moment they crossed the "deadline," a rail of pine logs running 25 feet inside and parallel to the fort's walls. Outside, cannons were pointed at the prison walls. According to Union soldiers who testified for the government during his trial, Wirz had often said that if just one man escaped, every Union soldier would be starved for it. Throughout the trial, however, Wirz maintained his innocence.

He was only following orders, he said. In fact, he had even written a letter detailing the need for more food. His defense, however, ultimately proved underwhelming. He was found guilty on November 6 and sentenced to die on the 10th in Washington, to hang in the same yard as had John Wilkes Booth.

He was hanged in front of an audience of Union soldiers chanting, "Wirz, remember Andersonville." They

If Andersonville inmates passed a fence called the "deadline" (lower right-hand corner), they could be shot on sight.

continued to yell at the man even as he twisted in the wind, taking over two minutes to die.

Andersonville was allowed to fall into ruin. But there were some who refused to let its memory fade too. Civil War nurse Clara Barton and Andersonville survivor Dorence Atwater knew that in forgetting the past, it shall be repeated. While in Andersonville, Atwater had compiled a list of the buried dead. Through the efforts, only 460 of the over 12,000 dead at Andersonville met their makers nameless.

Andersonville remembers the prison too. After all, the prison was recently restored and is now a national historic site open to all who are interested in the darkness of human suffering. In Andersonville itself, the man around whom so much controversy still swirls is hailed, by some, as a hero. Two monuments and a small museum in the town are dedicated to Henry Wirz. The different ways in which to view this man have extended into his haunting.

While most agree that Wirz has been seen numerous times walking around the ruins of the old fort, they argue why he might still be in Andersonville. His ghost is seen walking around the ruins, but some say he is trying to provide food and water to the prisoners as he did in life. Others argue that he is trying to atone for his viciously cruel past. At other times, he walks down the road leading to the Andersonville National Historic Site, never able to escape the carnage that he might have had a hand, intentional or not, in creating. He seems much more fortunate than the other ghosts present.

When the fog is thick at Andersonville, it seems to awaken something in the land and air. The groans, screams and cries of tortured and dying men can be heard coming in and fading out of the fog. The effect is, understandably, disorienting and unnerving. Once heard, the cries probably never leave the head. And from the ground, a foul and disturbing odor rises up. Some have said it's a smell reminiscent of field hospitals in the Vietnam War but much, much worse. So thick that some believe that they could choke on it and so strong that it assaults their senses with all the physical power of a punch, the stench is believed to be that of the Andersonville dying and dead, rotting away in their own accumulated filth. Mercifully, the odor fades as quickly as it appears. Through it all, the ghost of Henry Wirz walks.

To be sure, he cannot be the only one held accountable for what happened at Andersonville, but, unfortunately, he is. Surely there were other men who contributed to the horrific conditions at the prison. One can only hope that their spirits are trapped somewhere on this corporeal plane, paying penance for their misdeeds. Andersonville remains as a reminder of human atrocity and as a memorial to those interred within. Fittingly, Andersonville is also home to the National Prisoners of War Museum, a memorial to all Americans captured in all conflicts.

The Public House
ROSWELL, GEORGIA

Before the Public House became one of the more celebrated restaurants in Roswell, Georgia, it went through a number of permutations. The building has served variously as a commissary for the Roswell Mill, a general store and a funeral home. It has stood almost from the time that Roswell was founded in the early 19th century. Little wonder, then, that the Public House is as much a historical artifact as it is a restaurant. The building is heavy with the scent of history and folklore. It's palpable and tangible, writ for all to see in the cobblestone floors and brick walls that are original to the building. And while some diners may come to the Public House to dine on tuna or pork tenderloin, others come hoping to catch a glimpse of Michael and Katherine. It's not an easy task, for Michael and Katherine have been dead for over 140 years.

Mary-Alison Wilshire doesn't know if the stories about Michael and Katherine are true, but she is certain that spirits not found on any menu still haunt the Public House. It's been four years since Mary-Alison worked as a hostess at the Public House, but she can still recall with vivid detail the strange events she heard about and those that she witnessed for herself.

"Just standing in there," she says, "you kind of felt like you were never by yourself. Most of the people who worked there were used to hearing weird things."

One of the first things that Mary-Alison heard when she first began working at the restaurant was how the building was haunted and who haunted it. The story was "kind of like an initiation" and it is, like the best stories, one about love. It's about how two young lovers found one another in the tempest of war only to have the war tear them apart.

During the Civil War, the Public House was used as a field hospital. In the hospital, 20-year-old Katherine worked as a nurse for the Confederacy. Death and suffering were her constant companions. She despaired as she asked herself where the beauty of life had gone and when had everything been consigned to flames of woe. Her job was to save men so that they might survive to kill again. The pitiful irony of her situation wasn't lost on her. She did her best to ignore her growing sense of futility and find hope in sharing a private joke, in the kiss of the summer wind and the touch of another human being. It was difficult at first, to be sure, but then, Katherine found herself taking care of Michael, a Union soldier.

Although she nursed him back to health, even when able, Michael didn't leave. He stayed in Roswell because he had found everything he could have ever wanted—he had found love with his Confederate nurse. Best of all, she loved him too, even if he had come into the hospital wearing not gray, but blue. And here their troubles began.

While Katherine was able to look past Michael's uniform, others were unwilling. They condemned the nascent affair when they learned of what was taking place between Katherine and Michael. They whispered about Katherine's betrayal on the streets when she walked by, and they cast accusatory glances at the pair even while they strolled about with their hands barely touching and eyes meeting for brief moments.

Katherine and Michael were far from oblivious, recognizing that theirs was an illicit love. They did their best to restrain themselves in public, but it was the stolen glances that gave them away. Treasonous—that's what people called the affair. People in Roswell couldn't believe that Katherine, the sweet and pretty young nurse they'd grown accustomed to seeing walk through the town square, had fallen in love with a soldier in the hated Union army.

At a meeting with her superiors, Katherine was told that the relationship would have to end. She could end it herself, but if she didn't, they would intervene. Katherine refused. From her love, she drew the strength necessary to bolster her resolve. But it was not enough. When her superiors realized that she had not ended the relationship and had no intention of doing so, they did what they had threatened and intervened. Michael was taken and, as Katherine watched from the second floor of the converted hospital to the square below, he was hanged for treason. Those who knew Katherine best say she never forgot Michael and how much she loved him. She often talked of how they would be reunited again in the afterlife. Should the rumors and stories be believed, it has happened. Katherine and Michael are together again.

"It would make perfect sense," says Mary-Alison. "Rumor has it that the lovers hide behind the walls during the day and come out and waltz together at night." While Mary-Alison never did see the waltzing couple, she did say that being upstairs was "a little creepy." Knowing the restaurant's history probably didn't help either. When it was used as a funeral home, coffins were lowered from the second to the first floor through an opening in the floor that is still there. The second floor now serves as the Public House's piano bar.

On one wall, two large chairs sit facing each other. Above them hang two very large oil paintings. One is of a man and the other is of a woman. While it's not known for certain whom the pictures represent, it's often surmised that these two paintings represent the star-crossed lovers and that it is from here that their spirits emerge to dance. Mary-Alison believes that there may be something to those stories.

"I sat in one of the chairs once," she says. "It felt so eerie and strange that I never did it again." Mary-Alison discovered over summer stints at the restaurant while on break from college that the chairs and the piano bar weren't the only places where strange things happened.

As hostess, Mary-Alison worked mostly afternoons. On occasion, however, she would work the evenings. On those nights, she would arrive for her shift at 5 PM, and, as she was usually the only female staff member, it was her responsibility to make sure that the women's restroom was well-stocked with such items as paper towels and toilet paper. One night, Mary-Alison went into the restroom and turned on the lights. She found everything satisfactory, and she left the room. She's certain that it couldn't have been more than five minutes before she returned to the restroom and found it plunged into darkness.

Odd, she thought. She could have sworn that she had turned on the lights, was certain of it in fact. For a second, she thought maybe someone else had gone into the room, but she was the only woman working. Could it have been a customer? No, that possibility was ruled out quickly. The restaurant was still closed and had yet to admit a single customer. Mary-Alison shook her head and turned the lights back on. She searched the restroom, but it was clear that she was the only person alive in the room. The realization had just dawned upon Mary-Alison when she heard something. With wide-eyed disbelief, she heard one of the toilets flush. If Mary-Alison ever had any doubts about the paranormal presences in the Public House, they had just been washed away.

"I was the only person in there," Mary-Alison described. "I think the ghost was playing tricks on me."

When Mary-Alison ventured to broach the subject of ghosts with her manager, he treated her not with skepticism, but with a knowing familiarity. He pointed to the portraits that hung on the wall of the main dining room.

He talked about how one morning staff had come into the Public House to find that all the portraits had fallen from the wall. Interestingly enough, none of the glass in any of the frames had shattered; it was as if someone had taken the time to remove the portraits from the wall and gingerly place them on the floor. Naturally, the restaurant was empty when any of these paintings could have been moved. The manager had made sure of it before he locked up and armed the security system. After all, if someone had broken into the building, the alarms would have been tripped. Or so he told himself. Because if that was what he believed, then what happened next must have come as quite a shock.

He described to Mary-Alison how he was wakened at four o'clock one morning by a phone call. It was the security company, calling to report that internal sensors in the restaurant had picked up movement. Oddly enough, though, none of the sensors mounted along doors and windows had gone off, suggesting that whoever or whatever was moving around inside must have hidden inside the restaurant before it was locked for the evening. The manager insisted that he had been the last to leave, that he had made a thorough check of the establishment and had found it empty. When he arrived at the restaurant, he was amazed to find pots and pans strewn over the floor and shards of broken glass littering the ground like sparkling confetti. How had it happened? The question kept running through his mind.

He checked all the doors and windows himself and everything was in order. After that, he carried out a thorough search of the building, looking into every dark corner and behind every door. Maybe whoever had tossed the pots and pans around was still in the restaurant, hiding. But the manager's exhaustive hunt turned up nothing. Whoever it was had vanished, but certainly had not left the restaurant.

Mary-Alison can still remember evenings when she would light the table candles in the main dining room, go upstairs and come back down only to find that all the candles had been blown out. She might have originally attributed their extinguishing to a draft, but the frequency with which it happened when there was no draft left Mary-Alison thinking there had to be something else at work.

So did the bartenders. Each night, before leaving, the bartenders cleaned the bar and then made sure that the wine bottles were arranged with their labels facing out. Most of the time, when they returned to work the following day, they would find everything in order. But every now and then, they would find that every one of the wine bottles had been turned around so that the wine labels faced not out, but in.

"All they could do," Mary-Alison says, "was just say, 'Well, it's happening again' and just attribute it to the couple." Sigh and shrug—it seemed that's all anyone could do when things in the Public House went awry.

Mary-Alison was at a complete loss one particular evening. As a hostess, she made sure that people waiting for tables were outfitted with a pager that vibrated and lit up when their table was ready. It saved her from having to yell out names or track down customers who might have wandered off somewhere. The pagers were meant to be a convenience. On this night, they were anything but.

"All of them began to go off," Mary-Alison recalls. "It was actually quite annoying. One would start and then the other and another and soon, they were all going off." The really interesting part of it all? When all the pagers started shaking and vibrating, Mary-Alison unplugged their cradles, hoping that disconnecting their power source would stop the pagers from going off. It didn't. Even unplugged, the pagers continued to alert customers.

Are the spirits of Michael and Katherine behind all the mischief? No one seems sure. Mary-Alison suspects that considering the building's history and past, it's not unlikely that other spirits might be at work in the Public House.

"It's kind of scary," Mary-Alison said when remembering another incident, "but it seems that kids can sense more." It's certainly a notion that was explored to great effect in such films as *The Sixth Sense* and *The Ring*, but Mary-Alison didn't need to see either of those movies to experience the phenomenon.

A woman had come into the Public House to book the second-floor piano bar for a Christmas party. Accompanying her was her five-year-old son. While the woman was shown around the room, her son played quietly in a corner of the room. Satisfied with her tour, the woman called out to her son and told him that they were going to go back home. He refused to leave. The woman told him again, her voice growing sterner. The child protested, saying that "he wanted to play with the soldier." The mother looked around the room. She didn't see a soldier. In fact, she had no idea whom her child might be speaking about.

"Honey," she said, gently, "what soldier are you talking about?"

The child proceeded to describe in exacting detail the uniform of a Confederate soldier.

"How could the kid know what a uniform looked like? He was five," says Mary-Alison. "He described things that wouldn't have been possible unless he actually saw the Confederate uniform."

If the story is true, it raises the question as to who else is living in the Public House along with Michael and Katherine. The child has seen a Confederate soldier; Michael fought for the Union. Certainly, as a Civil War hospital the building must have seen more than its fair share of death. And perhaps one or more of those soldiers stays behind in the corporeal world. Why? No one will ever know. But one does hope that the Confederate soldier knows to leave well enough alone and allow Michael and Katherine the love and happiness that was denied them in life.

Johnson's Island
SANDUSKY BAY, LAKE ERIE

In 1861, Secretary of War Simon Cameron assigned Lieutenant-Colonel William Hoffman to manage the new Federal prison system. As Commissary-General of Prisoners, Hoffman's first duty was to construct a prison immediately. The Civil War had not ended as quickly as people had hoped and a prison was necessary to house the thousands and thousands of Confederate soldiers that Union troops had captured and expected to capture in the coming months. Hoffman realized that his first task would not be an easy one.

The prison's site would have to be remote, to render escape all the more difficult and grant the Federal government more control over access to the facility. With these requirements in mind, Hoffman arrived in Sandusky along the northern Ohio shoreline in October 1861. A number of islands in Lake Erie held promise as potential sites, and Hoffman took to inspecting them aboard his ship, the *Island Queen*. He explored Middle and North Bass Islands but dismissed them for being too close to Canada. He felt that the relatively large civilian population on South Bass Island would resent the placement of a Federal prison so close to their homes. Construction would have also devastated the island's wine industry. Kelly's Island was considered for a moment and then rejected. Hoffman was growing more frustrated with each location he had to rule out and had grown weary of the search. But then, he chanced upon Johnson's Island.

Johnson's Island was perfect. It was just three miles north of Sandusky and far enough removed from the Canadian border. Its size and resources were appealing. At 300 acres, the island was heavily wooded, thick with stands of hickory and oak. When needed, the trees would provide a ready and plentiful fuel source; anything else that might be needed could be obtained from the mainland. Forty acres had already been cleared and the site was well suited for construction. Most importantly, the cold and harsh conditions of a Lake Erie winter would be alien and hostile to Confederate soldiers long accustomed to the warmer and sunnier conditions of their Southern homes; the extreme weather would prove overwhelming to those with less than sturdy constitutions.

A lease was negotiated with L.B. Johnson for $500 a year. Johnson was thrilled that the government was going to clear his land, thereby increasing its agricultural and limestone quarrying value at no cost to him. After all, there was potential profit to be had after the war. To everyone involved, it was a perfect arrangement. Johnson filled construction contracts for the prison 30 days after his first arrival on Johnson's Island.

Sandusky builders William T. West and Philander Gregg won the contract and they constructed the grounds' initial buildings for $30,000. By the middle of February 1862, the prison was completed, with enough room to house 2500 men. On April 11, 1862, the prison accepted its first prisoners, transfers from Camp Close, 200 Confederate soldiers ferried across Lake Erie on the *Island Queen.*

Their world was now just over 16 acres, consisting of a stockade with 13 two-story blocks, 12 of which were used for prisoner housing. A 15-foot high wooden fence made sure that the prisoners wouldn't stray. Each block was thick with the stench of waste that failed to drain properly from the privies. The smell seeped in through the gaps that appeared in the walls as the green lumber used in the blocks' hasty construction shrunk as it cured and dried. The prisoners found small relief from the stench when they were able to cook. Each block had a kitchen at one end with a cast iron stove, and it was here, when water was available, that they laundered and cooked and pre-pared meals for other prisoners. The menu was limited, of course, ranging from salted fish or pickled beef in a rice and bean stew. It was a hard life, and although some pris-oners considered escape, it was never really an option. Certainly, there were those who tried. They attempted to dig through the latrines and out beyond the stockade walls but found their progress halted by thick dense layers of limestone.

The 128th Ohio Volunteer Infantry was the official guard of the prison. Two major forts, Fort Johnson and Fort Hill, were built over the winter of 1864 and 1865 to protect the island and were fully operational in March 1865. Anchored just offshore was the gunboat *Michigan*. Her guns were aimed permanently at the prison walls and the sight of the cannons' gaping maws must surely have been disheartening for any prisoner considering escape. If that fearsome sight did not break their spirits, then there was the fact that any prisoner attempting to flee to Canada faced a 30-mile swim across the forbidding waters

Eyewitnesses on Johnson's Island have seen ghosts of Confederate soldiers rise out of their graves.

of Lake Erie in the summer months and a frozen trek in winter. Those daring the feat found that the comforts of the prison, while small, were sorely missed.

The first wardens at the prison were known for their harshness and cruelty, unable to separate their prisoners from the uniforms that they once wore. To keep the prisoners demoralized and beaten, rations were restricted and the soldiers were gradually denied anything that might have allowed them to feel free. William S. Pierson, the first warden, was replaced because of how badly he treated the prisoners and because he was inept at handling even simple administrative problems. On January 18, 1864,

Brigadier General Harry D. Terry became his replacement. Terry lasted until May, when Colonel Charles W. Hill took over the position and remained in charge until the war's end. While the prisoners always welcomed a warden who might be kinder and gentler than his predecessor, there was little they could do about weather, disease and the combined stresses of war and captivity.

The gaps in the block walls allowed the cooling lake breezes into the hot and humid blocks but in winter admitted the icy blasts of winter's breath. Prisoners stuffed newspapers and whatever other material they could scrounge up into the cracks and holes to create a crude form of insulation. Often, it wasn't enough to keep back the frigid air or the pneumonia and fevers that often followed when prisoners were weakened by the cold. It's alleged that close to 300 prisoners died at Johnson's Island prison. All of them were buried in a small cemetery at the north end of the island.

Johnson's Island was in operation as a prison for almost four years. During that time, more than 10,000 officers and 1000 enlisted men were imprisoned on the island. When the war ended, prisoners were finally released and sent home, save for those buried in the cemetery. While surviving prisoners were treated to warm homecomings, the dead had their wooden grave headboards replaced with Georgia marble. Given the chance, most or all of those buried at Johnson's Island would probably like to be moved elsewhere, perhaps someplace closer to their homes and far from the site of so much suffering. Even now, so many years later, there are those who swear that the dead of Johnson's Island continue to protest their fates.

It's been written that in the early 20th century, laborers in Sandusky Bay were quarrying stone one late fall. Weather can change rapidly in the Midwest, and blue skies were quickly replaced with big black rolling clouds. The air cracked and split with the rumbling of thunder as lightning arced across the sky. The laborers ran for the closest shelter: the wooded groves of the Johnson's Island cemetery. It was here, huddled beneath the branches, that the men saw a sight never seen before on the island. Amid an eerie green light, figures were rising from the graves, coming together to form something that hadn't been witnessed since the end of the Civil War almost 50 years before—a company of marching Confederate soldiers. As the men would later report, the ghostly soldiers fell into formation and began a march home across the bay.

More recently, visitors have experienced an overwhelming sense of dread as they walk the cemetery grounds, and others have heard the very faint strains of Dixie, the Confederacy's anthem, in the air. The war may be over, but the past continues to echo.

5
Gettysburg

Ghosts of Gettysburg

Before the Civil War, little about the town of Gettysburg distinguished it from any other small municipal settlement in the state of Pennsylvania. A small rural town that largely relied on the surrounding agricultural activity for subsistence, the borough was most known for its location at the hub of six highways. But that would change on the morning of July 1, 1863, when two Confederate brigades, tired, hungry and in bad need of supplies, crested Herr Ridge, a promontory that overlooked the sleeping town.

Brigadier Generals James Archer and Joseph David had no idea they would be initiating the deciding battle of the Civil War when they ordered their units to occupy the town. The Union forces defending Gettysburg put up what resistance they could against the advancing Confederates, but spent much of that fateful morning staging a fighting withdrawal from the superior numbers on the Southern side. The scale of the engagement increased dramatically as the Confederates pushed through the streets of Gettysburg. It began as a minor battle between two relatively small groups of combatants, but reinforcements from both sides continued to arrive as the day wore on, with the last soldiers marching into the area just before midnight. The next morning saw General Robert E. Lee's entire Army of Northern Virginia, 75,000-strong, arrayed just south of the town of Gettysburg, glaring across at General George G. Meade's 97,000-man Army of the Potomac.

By then, it was obvious to everyone that something terrible was about to happen. And it did. The numbers

Many ghosts have been spotted at Little Round Top, the site of a pivotal engagement during the Battle of Gettysburg.

speak for themselves: from July 1 to July 3, the roaring machinery of the Civil War claimed over 50,000 American lives, making Gettysburg the bloodiest battle of the four-year conflict—indeed, the bloodiest battle the Americans have ever endured in any war to this very day.

Measured by the sad scales of human tragedy, the losses incurred at Gettysburg dwarf those of any other battle in American history. While the United States military has weathered more than one tragedy since its inception, the horrors of D-Day, Pearl Harbor, Antietam or any other engagement do not match, by sheer volume, the unforgiving brutality of Gettysburg.

Given the facts, is it any wonder that Gettysburg is considered the most haunted place in the United States? When a single untimely death may cause a disgruntled spirit to haunt an area for any number of years, what happens when tens of thousands lose their lives in the staggering horror of battle? It could be the sheer trauma of the events leading to death; the lasting acrimony of those soldiers reluctant to give their own lives for abstract political ideals; or the incredible historical significance of soldiers' actions as they wrestled over the battlefield for those three days. Whatever the case, Gettysburg today is replete with the spirits of men who fought there over 100 years ago.

Among all the bizarre occurrences that have been witnessed in the National Military Park, the supernatural sightings on Little Round Top and Devil's Den have received the most attention. It was around these two structures, located at the southernmost limits of the fighting, that much of the battle's most critical combat took place.

Little Round Top, a forested hill that loomed over the Union line's left flank, was a valuable strategic location for the Confederate forces *and* the Union army. If the Confederates were able to take the high ground on Little Round Top, their elevated position over the southern Union lines could very well shatter General Meade's entire flank and secure victory for the rebels. So it was imperative to the Union strategy that their left flank be anchored with a strong defensive position on Little Round Top. But the Union command had initially overlooked the importance of the hill and had left it virtually unoccupied, instead positioning the left flank of the

Union army on rocky ground near the base of Little Round Top—a boulder-strewn stretch of land known as Devil's Den.

It was here that the Confederate attack on the Union left flank began. The fighting for Devil's Den was fierce and bloody, raging back and forth for much of the day. Sharpshooters nesting behind the massive boulders traded lead with each other as lines of infantry advanced, took over, retreated and then advanced again over what had become a bloody outcropping of rocks. The seesaw battle ended with the Stars and Bars waving over Devil's Den, and thousands of battered and bloodied men from Georgia and Texas standing among nearly as many dead.

The legendary assault on Little Round Top began soon after the Confederates attacked Devil's Den. Union command became aware of the imminent danger Little Round Top posed to their position when a Union engineer on lookout became suspicious of the hill's heavily wooded southern slope. He ordered a shell to be fired into the area and was startled to see the sudden gleam of countless gun barrels and bayonets. There was no mistaking what he saw in the trees—an enormous body of Confederate infantry poised to make the ascent up the suddenly strategic hill.

Immediately aware of what a Confederate movement would mean to the Union position, the officer relayed a desperate message to General Meade, who ordered that the hill be defended at once. Brigadier General James Barnes arrived at Little Round Top just in time to greet the advancing Confederates, inaugurating what would become one of the decisive engagements of Gettysburg with a devastating volley of rifle fire. The enormous losses

By battle's end, the boulders of Devil's Den, another key position, were stained with the blood of many fallen soldiers.

suffered on both sides over the next few hours would transform Little Round Top from an anonymous hill rising out of the farmlands of southern Pennsylvania into the Alamo of the Civil War.

Wave after wave of Confederate soldiers rushed up the murderous slope only to be repulsed by the ever-decreasing line of Union men at the top. The hardest pressed regiment holding the crest of Little Round Top was the 20th Maine, led by the legendary Colonel Joshua Chamberlain. The 386 men in Chamberlain's unit guarded the southernmost tip of the entire Army of the Potomac.

Just before Chamberlain's superior officer galloped off to supervise the rest of the defense, he reminded the colonel of his incredible responsibility: "You understand. You are to hold this ground at all costs."

The regiment's onerous duty to protect the left flank was made even more difficult by the fact that the 15th Alabama charging up the hill was constantly threatening to outflank them. Stretched thin and running out of powder, the 20th Maine held off one charge after another, repeatedly sending the Alabama rebels into a retreat towards the base of the hill, where they would regroup and come again. With casualties mounting and their ammunition almost completely depleted, the situation was turning desperate for the 20th, when Colonel Chamberlain gave the order that would win him the Medal of Honor.

"Fix bayonets!" the colonel yelled over the roar of gunfire and cannon.

As incredulous as the order seemed, every soldier along the line knew that it was about to get worse: their colonel intended to order them out from behind their covered positions and charge the Confederates below. There were no surprises; that was precisely what he did. In the next moment, the seemingly suicidal command came down the line: "Charge!"

For an instant, it seemed as if the 20th would not be able to carry out this order, as the men balked before the sight of the Alabama regiment below. But the bravery of a single lieutenant, who obeyed the command without any hesitation and charged down the slope alone, challenged the courage of each and every man at the top of the hill. A few seconds later, the 20th Maine was charging down the southern slope of Little Round Top, Colonel Chamberlain leading the way. They had no way of knowing it, but the redoubtable Chamberlain was leading them to glory.

The suddenly aggressive move caught the Confederate regiment completely off guard, and they reeled under the onslaught of the surprise counterattack. After a few harried moments of hand-to-hand combat, the Alabama regiment broke, retreating from the hill with the sound of the cheering Union men behind them. Colonel Chamberlain and the 20th Maine had saved the Confederate flank.

The extraordinary counterattack of the New England regiment that day was matched only by the extraordinary scope of the slaughter. Dead men, both Union and Confederate, were littered across Devil's Den. The narrow gulch that dipped down between that rocky battlefield and Little Round Top was so choked with the bodies of fallen soldiers that it became known as the Valley of Death from that day onward. And the slopes of Little Round Top itself were virtually blanketed by the bodies of the slain.

The Confederate attempt on the Union left was thwarted, and the next day, the hottest fighting moved north along the line. A few weeks later, all that remained in the area were memories of the brutality of that July 2 day—memories that were determined not to be forgotten.

It is difficult to say who saw the first ghosts around Little Round Top. One popular legend has the men of the 20th Maine spotting the spirit of none other than George Washington on the day of the battle. According to this tale, it was the sight of his bold image, standing before the regiment's line with sword raised towards the enemy, that inspired the wavering men to make their daring attack down the side of Little Round Top.

Whether or not the spirit of George Washington would be so roused by the fighting as to return from the grave and lead the beleaguered men of the 20th into battle is open to speculation. But as romantic as the supernatural legend is, there are no surviving firsthand accounts of veterans claiming to have seen the towering first president leading them forward with a raised sword. Certainly no one since the battle of Gettysburg has said anything about a specter of George Washington marching down Little Round Top.

Yet while George Washington seems to have retreated quietly back into his grave, it seems that many of the men who died on the southern reaches of the great Civil War Battle have been unable to find their own resting places.

All sorts of bizarre incidents have been reported around Little Round Top over the years. Visitors to the park who have lingered on the hill late into the day have been treated to eerie displays. During the early hours of clear, cloudless nights, thick mists have suddenly formed around the hill, rising in thick tendrils from the ground where thousands fell. From within this thick fog, people standing at the top of the hill have witnessed long lines of numerous flashing lights coming to life on the terrain below. These lights do not flash only once, nor do they remain still. For those standing and watching have claimed that the flashes continue at regular intervals, starting small, as if coming from a distance, and getting slightly larger with each consecutive illumination. By the time the lights flash for the final time, they appear to be no more than 30 yards from the witnesses at the summit of Little Round Top—and then they are gone. While no one can say for sure, most people believe that the recurring phenomenon is a supernatural reenactment of the Confederate advance on Little Round Top.

On other occasions, people have spotted a transparent horseman dressed in a Union officer's uniform astride a phantom steed. The horse picks its way down the side of the hill with slow, careful steps—as if the ghostly beast is conscious of the fact that the officer on its back is headless and unable to choose a path for himself.

But one of the most frequently occurring phenomena in that area involves cameras. As Gettysburg is a popular tourist destination, millions of people with cameras of every type have descended on the location at one time or another, snapping pictures or recording videos of the famous battleground. While some mechanical difficulties would certainly be expected, especially given the number of people that have visited, the nature of some of the malfunctions have been a little too freakish to be casually disregarded.

Many visitors have found that their cameras have inexplicably jammed up when they tried capturing certain areas on camera. This especially seems to happen in places where there were particularly high concentrations of casualties. Brand new cameras have mysteriously stopped working when used to take pictures of the Valley of Death. Many people attempting to take pictures here have had their cameras simply freeze up. Film will suddenly be unable to load, shutters won't open or batteries will go dead. While many of these individuals get angry that their equipment is not functioning, others claim to feel a cold, uncomfortable sensation, as if they aren't welcome in the spot where they're standing. Yet when these people walk away from the area, the feeling disappears and their equipment begins to function normally again.

Out among the massive boulders of Devil's Den, a completely different type of camera-related phenomenon has been said to occur. Tourists looking for the perfect shot to tuck into their photo albums have reported the appearance of a scraggy-looking young man, barefoot and dressed in patched clothing, with a big floppy hat sitting atop long brown hair. Speaking with a thick Southern drawl, he often gives photographic advice to people who are puzzling over shadow and light. "There's yer shot," he'll say, pointing towards one cluster of boulders. People who can't seem to choose what area deserves celluloid preservation have turned around to find themselves face-to-face with this young man. "How 'bout them rocks over there?" he suggests helpfully.

The advice he gives is almost always taken, but when the photographers turn to thank the young man for his help, they are surprised to see that he has disappeared as quickly and quietly as he came. Park managers have heard more than one inquiry about the "helpful young hippie in Devil's Den."

There are those whose experience among the boulders eliminates the possibility of mistaking this man for a free-spirited flower child. These are the tourists who do not see the man until weeks after visiting, when they are looking through their photographs of the battlefield. He appears in the pictures of Devil's Den, sometimes faintly, sometimes much more discernable, staring blankly at the photographer. What shocked most people about the appearance of this lone celluloid image was not the long hair, big hat, rough clothes or bare feet but that the man wasn't there when the picture was taken.

This phantom has come to be recognized as the Confederate ghost of Devil's Den. Why he has chosen to stay behind is anybody's guess, and why he seems to have taken an interest in the art of photography is just as mysterious. Perhaps he was a man who once had a deep appreciation for the landscape and has remained behind in Devil's Den to help others capture the natural beauty of the place. Or maybe he was one of those whose death came so suddenly and so violently that some part of his soul is unable to recognize that he is gone, so he still hangs around the site of his demise, making himself useful any way he can.

The ghosts covered here are just a small sample of the paranormal activity that goes on in Gettysburg. Numerous revenants have been sighted over the years in the area, from the bloody ground of the infamous Angle to the legendary Wheatfield. Given the staggering loss of life that occurred around the once-innocent little Pennsylvania town, we can only expect such devastation might leave an impression on the place. The living have continued to recognize the immense sacrifice that took place on that battlefield with all the monuments, reenactments and history lessons that center on it. As for the dead, it seems that they, too, seem intent on making sure that people don't forget what happened during the first three days of July 1863. And odds are that visitors to the

Gettysburg National Military Park—the most haunted place in North America—will have a better chance of witnessing a supernatural phenomenon there than they would anywhere else on the continent.

Gettysburg Tour

Close to the urban metropolises of Philadelphia, Washington, D.C., and New York City, but far enough that its bucolic splendor remains unspoiled, Gettysburg remains a popular destination for families looking to escape the tangles of the concrete jungle. Over 1.8 million people make the pilgrimage to this hallowed ground each year, seeking to steep themselves in a history that can never be forgotten and whose tremors are still felt all across the United States. Here Lincoln delivered his Gettysburg Address, the Confederacy was at its apex and the Union finally turned the tide of the war. To walk the verdant sun-drenched fields of Gettysburg is to journey into the past, to see where we have been and maybe get a sense of where we're going. History is resurrected, but there are forces other than tour guides and historical markers at work here that help to bring the past to life.

As much as historical interpreters and guides do to make Gettysburg's history as immediate and urgent as possible, their plaques and notes don't compare to the countless spirits of fallen soldiers who still walk the grounds of Gettysburg. Take a ghost tour of Gettysburg and the stories of the undead will rise up thick, like mist from a lake. While some might question the truth behind some of the stories, most undoubtedly have their roots in the folklore that began to spread almost as soon as the last of the battle's cannon fire had echoed its way across the fields.

Amanda Byrne has heard most of these tales, and while some embark on a ghost tour simply for a good fright, Amanda goes to see if she can make more sense of the strange and eerie sensations she feels every time she goes to Gettysburg. Raised in Selinsgrove, a town just two hours away from Gettysburg, Amanda has been to Gettysburg often.

Amanda doesn't question her particular sensitivity; she just accepts it. It was a gift she discovered one New Year's Eve while on a sleepover at a friend's house. She was already familiar with the house's resident ghost, Drew, but that night, she found herself idly wondering what the ghost's real name was and where he had come from.

It's a mystery whose answers don't appear to be forthcoming, but the moment she had asked herself those questions, Amanda heard the answers in her head. The spirit claimed to be Andrew S. Brown, a Dutchman from Lancaster who died in the 18th century. When Amanda told her friend what had happened, her friend nodded excitedly. In the basement, the friend often heard the voices of unseen people speaking what sounded like Dutch. In fact, Amanda's friend had taken to calling her ghost Drew. It was obvious to Amanda now. The voice she had heard in her head must have belonged to Andrew S. Brown; he was most likely one of many Dutch who settled in Lancaster. In Gettysburg, when Amanda wants to know about the battle, she doesn't ask the tour guides. The answers seem to present themselves.

Once, Amanda was standing atop Devil's Den with her church group, and one of the members asked the pastor leading the tour how many rows of soldiers marched in the line that advanced up the hill. Before the pastor could even answer, Amanda heard a voice say 12. Like an echo, the pastor's answer followed. He said 12.

Amanda first went to Gettysburg eight years ago, when she was a child.

"Even then," Amanda writes, "I could feel the presence of ghosts. All through Gettysburg, there is a certain presence." Last year, Amanda went on a ghost tour of Gettysburg and while some might have the found the stories amusing, Amanda saw them as validation for the chill she felt deep within her bones. As they walked through the town and stopped at various locations, Amanda felt the chill ebb and flow like a wave and knew that regardless of what stories the guide was telling, there was a paranormal presence somewhere close by.

"In areas where something major happened," Amanda explains, "I have a stronger feeling. This may sound crazy, but it's almost like I can talk to them. I can stand in a haunted area and ask a question and I can hear the answer in my head."

While she was on the tour, she felt odd—not scared or anxious, but just odd and a little apprehensive. She would soon understand why.

The tour stopped in the shadow of a hill and as the guide told the story of a Confederate soldier's last stand at Gettysburg, Amanda looked behind her. All she saw was

Historical engraving of Union soldiers on Little Round Top

the hill and some trees, but she sensed something coming from the area and was filled with a gnawing sense of unease.

The story, as Amanda remembers it, concerned a Confederate soldier who was determined not to let the Union army leave Gettysburg without a reminder of the persistence and will of the Confederacy. He commandeered a local family's home and despite pleas from others not to do it, he fortified himself on a second-floor balcony, threw up an oak table as a shield and began firing at Union soldiers from across the street. The Confederate soldier obviously hadn't thought his plan through.

The Union troops beneath him returned fire and under their steady barrage of gunfire, the oak table began to splinter away. With cover and ammunition both in short supply, the Confederate soldier was an easy mark. A Union sharpshooter raised his rifle and shot a bullet into the Confederate soldier's chest. The Confederate fell to the ground; on the balcony he lay, gasping for breath as his blood soaked through his uniform and collected in a sticky pool beneath him. His stare grew glassy, his breathing grew more ragged and shallow until he drew air no longer. Those of his companions who had been wise enough not to engage the Union troops carried his body away, leaving the blood-soaked balcony in their wake.

The family that lived in the house had hidden themselves away in their basement for the duration of the conflict. When the guns had been silenced, they felt they could venture forth. They were shocked at what they saw on their blood-spattered balcony. The mother ordered her two children to clean up the congealed pools of blood, which they did. Yet when their mother came to inspect the job they had done, she was livid as she discovered that the deck was as much a mess as before. She ordered her children to wash it again and warned them against the perils of lying, especially to a mother. The children, standing there in their bloodstained clothes, were flabbergasted. What had happened?

Regardless, they set about cleaning up the pools of blood once more. And, once again, when they were finished, they called their mother to inspect their work. And, once again, the mother was furious to discover that the blood had not been fully washed away. She sent her children to their room and set about cleaning the blood up herself, muttering to herself about the ineptitude of youth. A little while later, she was finished. She stood in the fading light of the setting sun and admired her work. She allowed herself a self-congratulatory nod and went inside. But then a strange thing happened and with this strange thing, she realized that her children hadn't been lying to her at all.

As she walked by the balcony the following morning, the mother was stunned to see that the pool of blood had returned. She cleaned it again, only to see it return. As the days passed, the family realized that no matter how hard they tried, there was just no way that they were going to be able to rid themselves of the stain. The phenomenon frightened them so thoroughly that in the end, the family tore the tainted house down and moved away.

But although the home was removed from the land scape, something of the dead Confederate soldier remains. His ghost can still be seen, lurking in and around the trees that dot the hill. Those like Amanda, with more sensitive constitutions, can sense his presence when his ghostly form escapes the eye.

She's sure it was him she felt as she stood in the shadow of the hill. Leaves swayed gently in the caress of the summer breeze, but the chill in Amanda's bones persisted. She turned to look behind her but saw nothing; eyes can be deceiving, though, and Amanda is positive there was something there. A dog's strange behavior stands as her proof.

Walking next to Amanda was a man and his dog. As the dog passed into the shadow of the hill, it became agitated, barking loudly and fighting the restraints of its leash. It lunged again and again toward the spot where Amanda sensed the presence. The owner did his best to calm his pet, but the dog refused to stop barking. People in the group turned to see what was irritating the dog so but turned away when they saw that it was barking at what was apparently nothing. The dog only calmed down when the tour moved away from the hill. It got excited again at Devil's Den and the Jennie Wade House, sites where Amanda once again felt a familiar chill creep into her bones. When the tour finished, Amanda knew that she would never forget what happened that June afternoon in Gettysburg.

The Civil War ended 140 years ago, but it is very much alive in spirit at sites such as Gettysburg. For some, like the Confederate soldier, it seems as if the war will never be over; they are trapped on this mortal plane, destined, it appears, to be living artifacts who help to make a trip to the site an unforgettable one. That, in the end, may have been the point all along.

Reynolds' Request

Joan Bennet was stressed. She hadn't been sleeping well, unable to wrest her mind away from fear and doubt. A month into her fourth year of studies at the University of Michigan, and all visions of her future were evaporating before her very eyes. With her coursework completed, all that stood between Joan and her degree was one semester as a student teacher in Flint. Yet there she was, four weeks into her semester and she had yet to teach a single class. A strike had closed the schools.

"I was killing myself to get through this," Joan says. "I didn't know if I was going to get my school teaching in. If I didn't, I wouldn't graduate. I didn't want to go back [for another year], I just wanted out."

Stressed and depressed, Joan found that even when she stumbled into sleep, rest was still elusive. A dream haunted her. Too often, she would wake in the morning, unable to return fully to reality. For years, she had this same recurring dream; it started in the 1970s and didn't stop until the 1980s. But even though Joan has not had the dream for years, she has never forgotten it. It is always there in her mind, and it wasn't until recently that she was able to discover why.

In her dream, Joan was standing outside a two-level farmhouse. The top floor was old and weathered. Parts of the wall had collapsed, exposing the level to the elements. Through the gaping opening, Joan could see a painting. It was a rendering of a man and woman. The man stood to the woman's left, cradling her body with his right hand and holding her hand with his left. His hair was parted

East Cemetery Hill No. One at Gettysburg

crisply to the right. The woman stared out a window wist-
fully, unable to return the man's gaze. In her right hand,
she held a white handkerchief. Both of them were dressed
in Civil War dress; the man wore the dark blue uniform of
the Union Army; his cap rested on top of his gloves. She
wore a checkered dress, with a hoop skirt and a high neck.
Her hair was pulled back into a bun. As Joan stared at the
painting, she was certain that the figures in the painting
were asking for her help, that a tragedy had befallen them
and that she could set the wrong things right.

"If only I could get to the painting," Joan says. "It's all I
kept thinking. If only I could get to the painting, I could
set it right."

Joan did graduate from school and as she set about navigating her life in the real world, she never forgot the dream. From time to time, she would return to the painting she had seen and ask herself what it all meant. Of course, she hadn't the faintest idea how to solve the painting's riddle.

In 1997, Joan was retired and again, she wasn't sleeping well. The feeble light of the approaching dawn only underscored her sleepless night. It looked cold outside. Joan wondered if it was as cold as it looked and turned on the radio to find a weather report. But instead of the weather, she heard a man discussing the short career of Union Army General John Fulton Reynolds.

A Pennsylvanian West Pointer, Reynolds first came to prominence in the Mexican War. He returned to West Point as an instructor and commandant of cadets before the Civil War threw him back onto the front. He rose quickly through the ranks. Both his commanding officers and the men who served under him recognized that Reynolds was a splendid soldier. He was courageous, dedicated and possessed a finely honed tactical sense. Joseph Hooker called him "the ablest officer" under his command. He commanded the Pennsylvania Reserves as they fell to the Confederates at Second Manassas. In late 1862, he was given command of the First Corps of the Army of the Potomac, leading them into battle at both Fredericksburg and Chancellorsville.

With the Union campaign to subdue the Confederacy meeting one defeat after another, President Abraham Lincoln was casting about for a new general to lead the Army of the Potomac; he had grown weary of Hooker's leadership. There were many rumors about who would receive the appointment, but the name mentioned most often was Reynolds'. Reynolds rode to Washington to tell Lincoln that if offered the command, he would accept only if he were free to act when and how he saw fit. Washington's interference with his authority would not be tolerated. Lincoln could not make the offer, and George Meade became commander of the army instead.

Meade's first duty of business was to turn the Confederate Army away at Gettysburg. He gave Reynolds command of three corps. When Union cavalry encountered Confederates at Gettysburg, Reynolds rushed his corps to the front to help hold the Union position. At 11 in the morning, on the first day of Gettysburg, July 1, 1863, Reynolds was shot or struck with shrapnel. No one seems to know which, although a number of Confederate soldiers stepped forward to claim credit for the kill. Reynolds died almost immediately. As his men watched his lifeless body pass their positions, a pall fell over them. Union commanders realized that with Reynolds' death, they had lost one of their most capable general officers. Catherine May Hewitt, of course, lost much more.

Secretly, Hewitt and Reynolds had been engaged just before he reported to the Army of the Potomac in 1861. In Philadelphia, Hewitt, teary-eyed, promised Reynolds that she would not marry another if he were killed in battle. When she learned of his death, Hewitt was devastated and stayed true to her word. She entered a convent.

Joan listened to the story with great interest, and she found herself moved by the poignant and tragic story. Intrigued, Joan began to delve further into Reynolds' history. Who was this man in life? She couldn't quite explain it and didn't know how, but Joan just somehow knew that what she had just heard was directly related to her dream.

Joan decided to visit Gettysburg and found a number of markers dedicated to Reynolds' memory. A street that runs through the battlefield bears his name. In the Soldiers National Cemetery, Joan found herself staring up at the general himself, in the form of a bronze statue. She gasped when she found its features eerily familiar. Was the man from her dreams General Reynolds? She couldn't be sure just yet, but her certainty was growing. She learned from historical interpreters that despite all the markers and monuments commemorating General Reynolds, he was buried not in the Soldiers National Cemetery at Gettysburg, but in Lancaster, Pennsylvania. Odd, she thought.

Joan spent the rest of the day touring the battlefield, walking through Devil's Den, around the Round Tops and standing at the place where Pickett led his ill-fated charge. The history inspired awe, and Joan marveled at the possibility that she might have trod over the same ground as had Confederate General Robert E. Lee or Union General Joshua Chamberlain. The day at an end, Joan returned to Gettysburg town to browse its seemingly endless array of souvenir shops. Most were stocked with figurines, sweatshirts, baseball caps, ill-fitting reproductions of Union and Confederate caps, and an inexhaustible supply of belt buckles, buttons, ammunition and other artifacts dug up from the field.

She passed in and out through a succession of shops, not buying anything because nothing had really caught her eye. Abandoning her quest, Joan began to wander down the tree-lined streets of Gettysburg. The day was warm, with a slight breeze in the air, and Joan had no wish to return just yet to her room at her hotel. Joan turned down a street to escape the milling crowds of tourists and had just passed a shop window when she stopped walking. A chill passed through her body for she could not believe what she was staring at through the shop window. There, in a gallery, hung the painting that had haunted her imagination for so many years.

"Catherine's dress was a little different," Joan explains. "That was all. Everything else about that painting was almost identical to what I'd seen in my dream." By nature skeptical about such psychic phenomena as telepathy or ESP, Joan found herself reconsidering her opinions when she discovered that the painting had been painted in 1997, exactly 20 years after she had first seen it in her dreams. It was too wondrous and perplexing to be mere coincidence. Was there the possibility that forces beyond human comprehension had engineered the event? Why had Joan experienced the same vivid dream again and again for years only to have the dream stop suddenly and reappear, slightly altered, in the waking world?

Joan had no idea what to think. Once, she had believed that if she saw the painting she would know intuitively how to set the wrong thing right, but standing there staring at the painting, Joan hadn't the first clue as to what she should do. For the moment, she was content to chalk up the incident as another in a long line of sublimely perfect coincidences for which life is known. It was all she could do.

Joan's mysterious connection to John Fulton Reynolds was sharpened by visiting monuments such as this Gettysburg memorial.

She returned to Michigan, puzzling over what had happened in Gettysburg. There had to be something that she could do. She was sure of it. Not long after, Joan began noticing that Catherine May Hewitt's name and her story kept coming up.

"It was like I'd stubbed my toe and kept stubbing it over and over again," Joan says. It was inexplicable to Joan, but by this point, she'd decided not to wonder why but instead, turned her attention to Catherine Hewitt. Who was this woman? Who had she been in life? The more Joan reached towards the past, the farther it retreated. Catherine's was a life of mystery. All Joan could

206 Ghost Stories of the Civil War

discover was that after she learned of Reynolds' death, she joined a convent. Five years later, she just disappeared, vanishing from the historical record. She learned little of her background, but after speaking with historians, she discerned that Catherine probably suffered through a hard life. In all likelihood, Catherine's only source of happiness was John Reynolds and the prospect of their marriage. With his death, her life faded. And it was then that Joan realized what it was she was supposed to do.

It was an epiphany. Joan was going to find Catherine. "I'd like to find her and get her buried with Reynolds. Bury them both under his statue in the Soldiers National Cemetery at Gettysburg," Joan said. "I feel as if they picked me to find her." Joan has yet to find Catherine; occasionally, she returns to Reynolds' grave in Lancaster to speak with him.

"I told him that he had to help me," Joan says. "But I get the feeling he wants me to work for it."

Retired, Joan dedicates most of her time to tracking down the woman. Already, she has come closer to uncovering Catherine's final resting place than anyone else, having uncovered an oversight here and an oversight there. It's appropriate work for Joan. Not only was she knowledgeable about American history, but also she feels that she must have been chosen for a reason, her skepticism about the supernatural notwithstanding.

"This story is my life now," she says. "The mystery came to me as a dream, but I will solve it." If Joan succeeds, John Reynolds and Catherine Hewitt will be reunited and will be together again at last, having spent over a century and a half apart.

The Farnsworth House Inn

During the Battle of Gettysburg, both sides suffered tremendous losses and the pain for the survivors was just beginning. Most fathers, mothers, brothers and sisters were able to convince themselves that their loved ones had not died in vain. They had died fighting for the Union or the Confederacy. But when death touched the innocent, such rationalizations proved elusive. So it was for Jennie Wade, the only civilian casualty of Gettysburg, and her family.

Gettysburg remembers Jennie Wade still. The proud daughter of fervent abolitionists, Jennie was in the kitchen baking biscuits for Union soldiers when an errant bullet from a Confederate sharpshooter struck her beneath her left shoulder blade and worked its way into her heart. Jennie fell to the ground dead. Desperate to invest her death with meaning, the United States Army ordered that an American flag be flown over her tomb, so that others might remember her contributions to the war effort. Her home at 758 Baltimore Street is a museum that bears her name. It is a shrine, looking almost exactly as it did on the day of her death. Indeed, the building from which she was shot stands still at 401 Baltimore Street. But, these days, it is populated not with Confederate sharpshooters as it was in 1863, but with tourists and Civil War buffs seeking good food, lodging and entertainment.

The building survives as the Farnsworth House Restaurant and Inn. Like many of the buildings in Gettysburg, the Farnsworth is a relic that breathes life into the distant past. Staring at its exterior, still riddled with hundreds of bullet holes, it's not hard to imagine a time when Jennie Wade might have passed freshly baked biscuits to Union troops hurrying through the streets to confront Confederate forces sweeping through the town. Such work was dangerous, as Confederate forces had taken possession of the Farnsworth on the first day of the Battle of Gettysburg. From the third-floor attic, Confederate sharpshooters controlled the perimeter of the base of Culp's Hill, exchanging gunfire often with Union troops. When the rebels finally fled from Gettysburg, the house, which had been built in 1810 and was home, at the time, to the Sweney family, became one of any number of general headquarters that the Union Army possessed.

The Farnsworth is proud of its ability to make the past immediate. Through its Mourning Theater, Candlelight Ghost Walks and Dinner Theater, the past comes to life. But for those who choose not to opt for their past to be translated through historical interpreters, just staying at the Farnsworth House Restaurant and Inn should be more than enough. The inn has 10 individually named rooms (not surprisingly, one of them has been named for Jennie Wade), and over half of them (McFarland, Catherine Sweney, Sarah Black, Jennie Wade, Garret Room and Shultz) are advertised as haunted. Temporary home to travelers and tourists, the Farnsworth is the permanent home for a host of spirits of the Gettysburg fallen.

By some accounts, there are as many as 16 different ghosts. Others put the number at a still-high 14. If you believe some of the stories, a ghost release ceremony was held at the home and while the restless spirits were given advice on how to escape the mortal plane, only two chose to go. Perhaps they are too comfortable with the inn and its rooms decorated with 19th-century antiques, fireplaces and whirlpools. Regardless, considering its role in the Civil War, it's not surprising that the Farnsworth House is regarded as one of the most haunted places in the United States.

Of the more than 10 spirits that haunt the Farnsworth House, the most talked about is probably Mary. She interacts frequently with guests, sometimes startling them from sleep when she sits on their beds. It's a favorite trick of hers. She's also fond of taking personal effects and hiding them from their owners. The items will usually reappear, but not until the living have become good and frustrated. On rare occasions, Mary will even materialize before guests. Despite her mischievous bent, Mary means no harm and visits people who are suffering and in pain, often lying down next to them in an attempt to comfort them. She has been known to usher away and chastise the ghosts that do mean harm.

The International Ghost Hunters Convention is held annually in Gettysburg. During the 2001 convention, members were taken on a tour of the Farnsworth House. They were escorted through all the bedrooms and different rooms, even the bathroom on the upper level that was reportedly closed because it is too haunted for the general public. People using the bathroom were too often treated to walls stained blood red. Apparently, a Confederate soldier bled to death there. In the attic, the ghost hunters were told the history of the house and the haunted accounts it had collected over the years. While there, participants described how four different spirits entered and left the room. One of them was described as being a "dark, negative male spirit" and anytime he entered the room, Mary, accompanied by the smell of roses, followed quickly to escort him away.

Mary works often to protect visitors from the negative spirit, a presence that some staff go as far to call bad and evil. He lurks, for the most part, in the catacombs that run beneath the Farnsworth House. Guests are discouraged, but not forbidden, from opening the door to the tunnels. Those who are too curious and who ignore the ominous warnings soon discover why they should have heeded the Farnsworth staff. Reaching for and touching the doorknob has been known to create a burning and stinging sensation in the hand. Inevitably, the door is left closed as stunned and surprised individuals run from the basement.

There is debate about who might be causing the sensation. Some say it's the evil trapped behind the door seeking to harm the innocent. Others point, once again, to Mary, the dedicated midwife in life and guardian in death. They'll point to the fact that the basement will fill with the scent of roses and lavender, her signature aromas. She creates the pain in the hand, so people are driven away before serious damage can be done. In the end, all one can really be sure of is that something lurks in the basement and that this spirit should be avoided. Mary does her best to make sure that happens. As for other spirits in the house, they still seem too concerned with their lives as they knew them to bother interacting with guests.

Jennie Wade, the only civilian casualty of Gettysburg, is one of many spirits at the Farnsworth House Inn.

Three spirits, believed to be Civil War soldiers, have been sighted on numerous occasions running through the building. One appears to be wounded badly, requiring help from his two companions to support him as he lurches clumsily across the floor. As their steps falter under the wounded man's weight, the other two soldiers, their faces marred with grimaces, call out for help. Even when someone has stopped and attempted to offer his or her assistance, the soldiers just stagger on down the hall, eyes fixed on points beyond the walls and doorways. How long will the soldiers continue to try to find help for their fallen comrade? Considering that the Civil War elapsed over a century and a half ago, it's reasonable to expect the soldiers to be a fixture at the Farnsworth House for at least a little while longer. They certainly won't be starved for company.

Guests arriving or leaving the inn should watch out for traffic on Baltimore Street lest they suffer the fate of another of the ghosts inside the Farnsworth House. Said to appear, sometimes together, are a father and his son. Given that one of the ghosts is a child, one can be assured that he met a most untimely and gruesome death. While playing, a boy was struck and trampled by a wagon. His father, who witnessed the accident, rushed to his son's aid. He took the child into the Farnsworth House where doctors worked frantically to save the child's life. The efforts were all for naught, however, and the child died, leaving a grief-stricken father to mourn his loss.

The father's grief is revealed for all to see when his spirit appears. Sometimes, the scene replayed shows the son still alive, cradled in his father's arms, and the anguish of a father raging at the fates is rendered all too clearly. At other times, it is too late and the father appears, aware that he has lost his child. One hopes that he might take some comfort in the fact that his son will still appear in front of the inn, playing in the streets. He's smiling and laughing, eyes twinkling and sparkling. But then, a transformation occurs. The smile and laughter fade, and the eyes open wide as the boy realizes that death is coming for him. While these two spirits don't acknowledge and seem unaffected by the other presences around them, they do touch those who witness them and learn their fates.

People who stay at the Farnsworth House Restaurant and Inn often come away with a wild and crazy story to tell. The Internet is full of stories from honeymooning couples and tourists who have posted accounts of hearing the sounds of battle near the Farnsworth House.

One couple visited the inn in 2000 for their honeymoon. Like many children growing up in the northeast, Miranda, the new bride, had been to Gettysburg when very young. She had been taken from the start by Gettysburg's welcoming and quaint atmosphere. Ian, her Canadian husband, had never been but was a Civil War fanatic. Their honeymoon seemed the perfect time to introduce and reintroduce themselves to Gettysburg's charms. Miranda and Ian, however, might have received a little more than they expected.

They passed the first couple of days of their stay walking the battlefield and exploring the shaded streets of the town. On the night before their departure, they decided to participate in one of the Farnsworth House's (in)famous ghost walks. A small group of about 10 or so, under the direction of a tour guide, began walking through the town. Every so often, the guide would stop and tell a story related to the particular location.

Near 11 PM, they were approaching the end of the tour and the guide came to a stop in front of the Farnsworth House, where she began to tell one last story. Miranda never heard it. Her attention was elsewhere, for off in the distance, she heard what she believed to be gunfire. She looked around but could see nothing. With night upon her, she untied her sweater from her waist and put it on, hugging herself. She looked around at the people standing outside the Farnsworth House with her but it seemed as if she was alone in hearing the gunfire. Everyone around her, even her husband, seemed to be watching the tour guide with rapt attention.

But when she caught the eye of a woman standing next to her, the woman leaned over and in whispered tones, asked Miranda, "Do you hear that too?" Miranda nodded, as if to speak would be to lose the moment. She squeezed Ian's hand, but he only turned for a brief moment to favor her with a small smile before turning back to the guide. How could he not have heard it, she wondered.

"Maybe it's kids playing with cap guns," the woman whispered to Miranda. Miranda nodded, but she was pretty sure that she was hearing gunfire. It was late, past many kids' bedtimes. Plenty of kids in her neighborhood back home were fond of cap guns and while they could be loud, they never even came close to sounding like this. She swore that she could even feel the earth moving beneath her feet, as if the Battle of Gettysburg were being waged all over again not even miles from where she stood.

Ian, as much as he was a Civil War fanatic, didn't believe in ghosts nearly as fervently, if at all. He wanted to believe Miranda, who insisted that she'd heard what she heard. What could he say? After all, he had heard nothing out of the ordinary, and the story was so odd. Finally, he told Miranda to write to the Farnsworth House, that maybe they would be able to help her understand the noises she had heard.

Miranda did write a letter to the Farnsworth House and a couple of weeks later, she received a reply. She was both thrilled and relieved to learn that she was not alone.

Her letter was among many that the Farnsworth House received each year from guests and tourists alike, each wondering what the gunfire was and each wondering why they had been the only ones to hear it. The letter comforted Miranda and she let Ian read it, just so he would know that he hadn't married a completely crazy woman.

Not all the letters deal with phantom gunfire, however. Some come from visitors eating breakfast in the inn's restaurant. Guests have reported hearing the laughter of children in the dining room, even when there are no children in the room. Could it have been children playing outside? Perhaps, but usually, when guests hear the children, all the windows in the dining room are closed. Who are these children? No one seems to know and any possible explanation would be a guess at best.

To be sure, though, the house is haunted. In a city like Gettysburg, where the past is what the present and future are built upon, the Farnsworth House is all but guaranteed to have a long and hopefully prosperous future. For as long as there are people who are fascinated with the afterlife or the Civil War, there will be more than enough people willing to make the pilgrimage to Gettysburg to pay homage to the fallen and with the justified expectations of seeing a ghost. At the Farnsworth House, they can do both.

Enjoy more terrifying tales in these collections by

GHOST HOUSE

GHOST HOUSE BOOKS

The colorful history of North America includes many spine-tingling tales of the supernatural. These fun, fascinating collections from **GHOST HOUSE BOOKS** involve well-known homes, public buildings and prominent landmarks. Collect the whole series!

Ghost Stories of the Old South *by Edrick Thay*
In this fascinating collection, Edrick Thay shows why the Old South is one of America's most storied regions. Explore centers of paranormal lore, such as Savannah, Charleston and New Orleans, or learn about stubborn yet genteel ghosts obsessed with the survival of Old Dixie.

$10.95US/$14.95CDN • ISBN 1-894877-18-7 • 5.25" x 8.25" • 200 pages

Ghost Stories of the Old West *by Dan Asfar*
The OK Corral, Fort Leavenworth, Billy the Kid, the Pony Express—the Old West had it all. Join Dan Asfar as he uncovers the charismatic ghosts who inhabit the prisons, forts and saloons where the Old West was born—and died.

$10.95US/$14.95CDN • ISBN 1-894877-17-9 • 5.25" x 8.25" • 216 pages

Ghost Stories of America, Volume 2 *by A.S. Mott*
Covering every region and era, A.S. Mott explores the nation's most infamous spirits, paranormal phenomena and haunted places, making this collection essential reading for skeptics and believers alike.

$10.95US/$14.95CDN • ISBN 1-894877-31-4 • 5.25" x 8.25" • 248 pages

Haunted Houses *by Edrick Thay*
With their blend of captivating history and ethereal residents, haunted houses have long been considered the most exciting haunted places. Edrick Thay reveals why in this eagerly awaited collection.

$10.95US/$14.95CDN • ISBN 1-894877-30-6 • 5.25" x 8.25" • 256 pages

Also look for
Ghost Stories of America *by Dan Asfar and Edrick Thay* ISBN 1-894877-11-X
Campfire Ghost Stories *by Jo-Anne Christensen* ISBN 1-894877-02-0
Haunted Theaters *by Barbara Smith* ISBN 1-894877-04-7

These and many more Ghost House books are available from your local bookseller or by ordering direct. In the U.S., call 1-800-518-3541. In Canada, call 1-800-661-9017.